Four Square

The Personal Writing Coach
for Grades 1-3

Writing and Learning Across the Curriculum

Written by Judith S. Gould & Mary F. Burke

Illustrated by Becky J. Radtke

Teaching & Learning Company

1204 Buchanan St., P.O. Box 10
Carthage, IL 62321-0010

This book belongs to

Cover photos by RubberBall Productions and PhotoDisc, Inc.

Copyright © 2005, Teaching & Learning Company

ISBN No. 1-57310-446-9

Printing No. 987654321

Teaching & Learning Company
1204 Buchanan St., P.O. Box 10
Carthage, IL 62321-0010

Table of Contents

Dear Teacher or Parent,

A teacher's biggest challenge is time. Between mandatory testing and the test preparation that goes with it and the few resources schools still have, there is precious little time for real instruction. Students with learning and behavioral disabilities bring with them additional challenges to the teaching day. Within any given day in school, there are also interruptions in the flow of instruction that provoke even the most saintly of our profession to near insanity.

Homeschool parent-teachers, we also understand your needs and concerns. Juggling domestic responsibilities and instructional duties is a daunting task. *The Personal Writing Coach* helps streamline instruction so even novice homeschooling parents will find it accessible and easy to use.

Our point is that we know all kinds of teachers and their struggles. The 13 themed units in *The Personal Writing Coach* will work with experienced writing students giving them many opportunities to play with language. *The Personal Writing Coach* will also help your reluctant writers by encouraging them into the process step by step, starting with artwork and progressing gradually to organized pieces of writing.

The process begins with drawing. Meshing the visual with the verbal is a natural first step in writing. It's especially good for reluctant writers who become anxious when it's time to write. Getting them to draw makes the physical action of putting pencil to paper less fearful because it is an already familiar activity.

Listing words in the Word Parade is the next logical progression after the artwork. Even though many children have complete thoughts derived from their artwork, jotting down words is less fearful than having to write full sentences. Some students may not need this activity, but chances are your reluctant writer will.

Repetition with basic and personal vocabulary will give the reluctant writer slow and steady experience with words. For the experienced writer, it provides opportunities to play with words by building on established language skills.

The poetry page is our personal favorite. A variety of poetic forms are included throughout *The Personal Writing Coach*. These help students create a piece of written work using their own words without having to worry about rhyming or meter patterns. These forms are not cast in stone. Teachers are encouraged to change the forms in ways that suit their lessons or add extra craft elements to the writing.

While the coach does not focus on mechanics (spelling, punctuation, grammar) in the activities, writers surely can choose to publish any of the drafts generated in the book in the form of a final, corrected copy.

The four square is a tool to help students who have never used a graphic organizer. We recommend that teachers model the four square and its connection to the actual writing which can be the final piece or just a rough draft. We've included an example on pages vi and vii to help you with your modeling.

This book contains 13 themed units, designed to meet the interests and abilities of your young writers. Each unit brings the prewriting through art, word association, questioning, form poetry, planning and finally composition of prose. Taking the themes through these same steps can help to build writer confidence and fluency.

Sincerely,

Judith Mary

Judith S. Gould
Mary F. Burke

Dear Writer,

This book is your personal coach for writing. Your writing coach, like a sporting coach is there to give advice and guide you. For each theme in this book, your coach has put together exercises to make your writing stronger. Use the coach to help your thinking and planning. Of course, the writing is up to you. Use your style and make the writing your own.

You can do these themes in any order, but you may find it easier to use the order your coach has provided. You may choose to make final, corrected, gorgeous copies of your writing or you may choose to leave it as a practice or scrimmage. Gear up with trusty pencils, erasers, crayons, markers and other sporting equipment and get ready to play!

Sincerely,

Judith Mary

Judith S. Gould
Mary F. Burke

Four Square

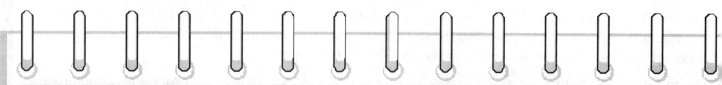

Where It Is

Right around the corner
Close by
I can walk
Brother walks with me

What I Do

Art supplies
Cool drawing
Dragon

After school I have so much fun at the Boys' and Girls' Club Center.

Friends That Are There

Alice
Likes to draw
Rainbows and teddy
   bears

Ending

Great place to be at the end of the day

That four square becomes this paragraph.
Notice how all the information stays on topic!

After school I have so much fun at the Boys' and Girls' Club Center. The Center is right around the corner from my school. I can walk there pretty easily, but my brother walks with me most days. When I am there, I like using the art supplies. Yesterday I made a cool drawing of a flying dragon with green and gold scales on the tail. My friend Alice also likes to draw. She always draws stuff like rainbows and teddy bears. We sit there together and talk and draw and before you know it, it's time to go home. Going to the Boys' and Girls' Club Center is the best way to end a day!

Four Square

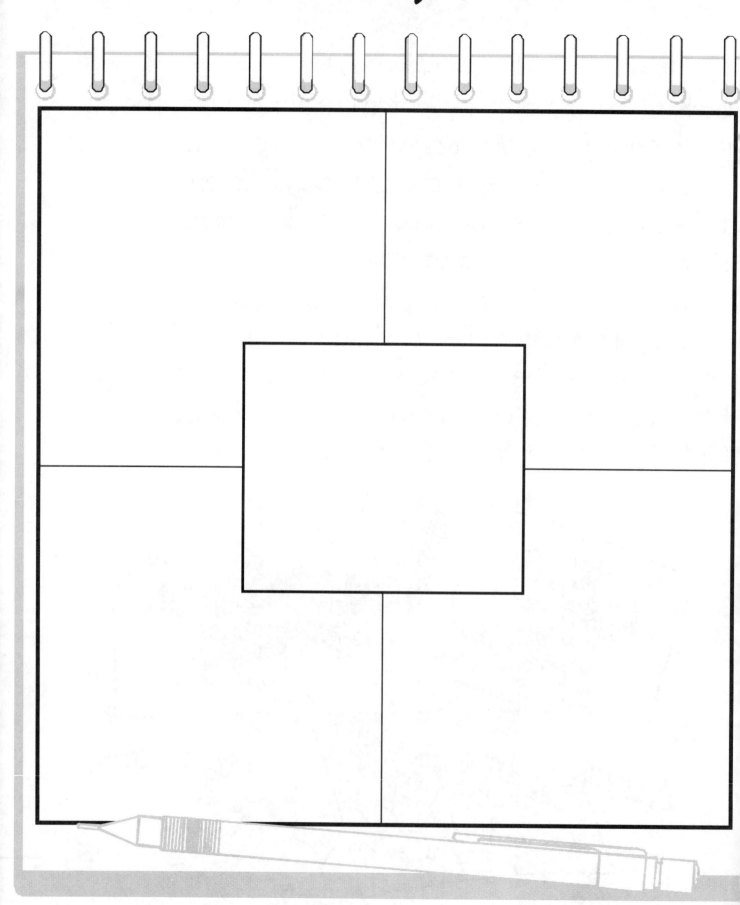

Section 1:
The Greatest Kid

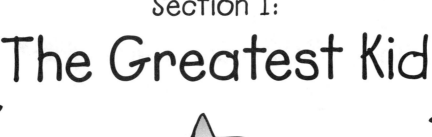

Who do you know the best?
Try writing about the greatest kid . . . you!
Don't worry, your coach will help you along.

Recommended reading for this project:

Leo the Lightning Bug by Eric Drachman and James Muscarello (Kidwick Books, 2001)
Stand Tall, Molly Lou Melon by Patty Lovell and David Catrow (G.P. Putnam's Sons, 2001)
Olivia by Ian Falconer (Atheneum/Anne Schwartz Books, 2000)
Amazing Grace by Mary Hoffman and Caroline Binch (Dial Books, 1991)

Name _____

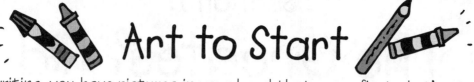 

Art to Start

Before you start writing, you have pictures in your head that come first. Let's start with those pictures! Get busy with your markers, colored pencils and crayons. Think about your writing while you are drawing.

Draw your face.	Draw your hands.
Draw your hair.	Draw your whole body.

ne _____

Word Parade

important to have words, and lots of them, parading in front of you before you start to write.
n you can pick them out when you need them. Let's start the parade by listing some words that
already in your head. Don't worry about spelling. You can fix that later.

Words that tell how you look

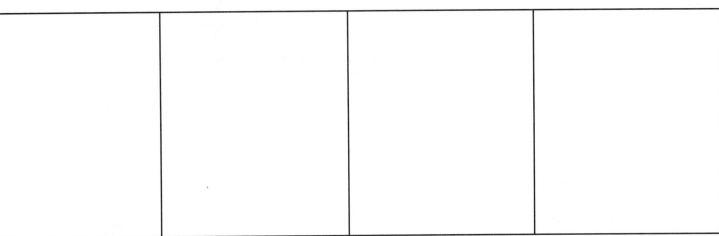

Words that tell what you wear

Name _____

Questions and Answers

Your coach would like you to think about your topic by answering these questions. Think of it as interviewing yourself!

1. Where do you have freckles? How many? More than 100? More than 1,000,000? _____
   _____

2. Is your skin the color of sand, chocolate or something else? Name it. _____
   _____

3. Does your nose go up or down? Is it the size of a button? An eraser? A bowling ball? _____
   _____

4. Are your ears flat or sticking out a bit? _____
   _____

5. Is your hair long or short? Is it straight or curly? _____
   _____

6. Do you spike your hair, or comb it neatly? _____
   _____

7. What kinds of clothes do you like to wear? _____
   _____

8. Do you like new shoes, or sneakers that get old and smelly? _____
   _____

9. Are you taller than the kitchen table? The back of the sofa? As tall as the roof of the car?
   _____

10. Who do you look like? A relative? Which one? A celebrity? Who?_____
    _____

12

Poetry

're ready to start writing. You have thoughts and words, you only need a way to get them
ether. Try using this poetry form. First spell your name down the side of the paper. Use a
ital for each letter, like this:

J

U

D

Y

n think of a word for each letter. It should say something about you. Maybe you will use the words
m pages 7 and 8 or you can think of others.

_____   _____

_____   _____

_____   _____

_____   _____

_____   _____

_____   _____

_____   _____

_____   _____

_____   _____

_____   _____

Name _____

Four Square

This will help organize your thoughts for writing to explain why you are proud to be you. Think of it [as] a map for your words and ideas so they don't get lost on the way from your head to the paper! In each of the squares, write words or phrases that go with the main idea of each box. Save your sen tence writing for later. Ready? Let's go!

2. Write two words to tell about how you look.

_____

_____

3. Write two words to tell about how you dress.

_____

_____

Use this sentence, or write your own beginning.

1. I am proud to be

_____

(your name)

4. Write two words to tell about who you are.

_____

_____

5. Now for your ending. I think I am a great kid because

_____

_____

_____

_____

A Word from Your Coach

The words in your four square will now form sentences for your writing, page 16.

Look at your four square and go to the middle box, #1. This will be the sentence that will start your writing. Go to your paper and start writing on the top line. Write a sentence with the words in this box.

Next, look at the #2 box. Make up sentences with the words in that box and write them on your paper. Make sure your writing is neat so your words can be read easily.

Go to the #3 box. Make up sentences with the words in that box. Do your sentences begin in different ways or do they begin with the same words (boring)? Write these sentences on your paper.

Go to the #4 box. Make up sentences with the words in that box. Do you use interesting and exciting words? Add these sentences to your paper.

Last, go to the #5 box. Choose an ending and write it down! If you haven't thought of a title, you might want to think of one. Add it at the top of your paper, above your writing. Now you're done!

You can do it!

Section 2:
The Relatives

Families can be big and far apart.
But let's think about your closest family.
These are the people you see almost every day or week.

Recommended reading for this project:

Families by Ann Morris (HarperCollins, 2000)

Arthur's Baby by Marc Brown (Little, Brown, 1990)

Celebrating Families by Rosemarie Hausherr (Scholastic, 1997)

Fathers, Mothers, Sisters, Brothers: A Collection of Family Poems by Mary Ann Hoberman
(Puffin, 1993)

Name _____

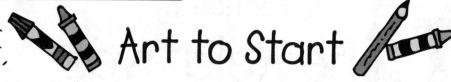 Art to Start

Before you start writing, you have pictures in your head that come first. Let's start with those pictures! Get busy with your markers, colored pencils and crayons. Think about your writing while you are drawing. Write the name of each person you draw.

Word Parade

important to have words, and lots of them, parading in front of you before you start to write.
n you can pick them out when you need them. Let's start the parade by listing some words that
already in your head. Don't worry about spelling. You can fix that later.

Name of person_____

Words

_____

_____

_____

_____

Name of person_____

Words

_____

_____

_____

_____

Name of person_____

Words

_____

_____

_____

_____

Name of person_____

Words

_____

_____

_____

_____

Questions and Answers

Your coach would like you to think about your topic by answering these questions. Think of it as interviewing yourself!

1. How many people live in your house? _____

2. How many living things are in your house that are not people? Plants? Pets? _____

_____

3. Do you share a room with anyone or anything? _____

_____

4. Who is the boss of the house? _____

_____

5. Who thinks he or she is the boss of the house? What does that person do? _____

_____

6. Who takes care of you? How? _____

_____

7. Who or what do you take care of? What do you do? _____

_____

8. Name other people living in your house. _____

_____

9. What are some of the special jobs everyone does at home? _____

_____

10. Is there someone really close to you who does not live in your house? Who? Where does that

person live? _____

_____

Poetry

…poem tells about your relatives. Just follow the form.

_____ is _____ and is my _____.
     (person)   (word that tells about the person)   (relationship to you)

…this as many times as you need for all of your relatives. For the ending use this: And I'm glad
…t we're related!

_____ is _____ and is my _____.

_____ is _____ and is my _____.

_____ is _____ and is my _____.

_____ is _____ and is my _____.

_____ is _____ and is my _____.

_____ is _____ and is my _____.

_____ is _____ and is my _____.

_____ is _____ and is my _____.

_____ is _____ and is my _____.

_____ is _____ and is my _____.

_____ is _____ and is my _____.

And I'm glad we're related!

Four Square

This will help organize your thoughts for writing to explain why a particular relative is special. Thi[nk] of it as a map for your words and ideas so they don't get lost on the way from your head to the paper! In each of the squares, write words or phrases that go with the main idea of each box. Sa[ve] your sentence writing for later. Ready? Let's go!

2. One reason: _____

_____

Detail about the reason:

_____

_____

3. Another reason: _____

Detail about the reason:

_____

_____

Use this sentence, or write your own beginning.

1. _____ is a very special relative of mine.

4. Another reason: _____

_____

Detail about the reason:

_____

_____

5. Now for your ending. How do you feel about this relative?

_____

_____

_____

_____

A Word from Your Coach

The words in your four square will now form sentences for your writing, page 24.

Look at your four square and go to the middle box, #1. This will be the sentence that will start your writing. Go to your paper and start writing on the top line. Write a sentence with the words in this box.

Next, look at the #2 box. Make up sentences with the words in that box and write them on your paper. Make sure your writing is neat so your words can be read easily.

Go to the #3 box. Make up sentences with the words in that box. Do your sentences begin in different ways or do they begin with the same words (boring)? Write these sentences on your paper.

Go to the #4 box. Make up sentences with the words in that box. Do you use interesting and exciting words? Add these sentences to your paper.

Last, go to the #5 box. Choose an ending and write it down! If you haven't thought of a title, you might want to think of one. Add it at the top of your paper, above your writing. Now you're done!

Let's get started!

My House

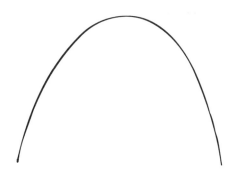

Some people live on farms in the country.
Some live in apartment buildings in a big city.
Wherever we live, our own home is a special place.

Recommended reading for this project:

The House That Jack Built by Diana Mayo (Barefoot Books, 2001)
Just Another Morning by Linda Ashman (HarperCollins, 2004)
There's a Nightmare in My Closet by Mercer Mayer (Puffin Books, 1992)

Name _____

Art to Start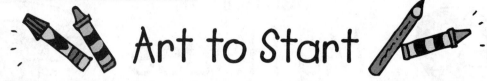

Before you start writing, you have pictures in your head that come first. Let's start with those pictures! Get busy with your markers, colored pencils and crayons. Think about your writing while you are drawing.

Draw the outside of your house.

Draw a map of the inside.

Draw your street or road.

Draw your favorite thing about your house.

Word Parade

Important to have words, and lots of them, parading in front of you before you start to write. you can pick them out when you need them. Let's start the parade by listing some words that already in your head. Don't worry about spelling. You can fix that later. Stand in one room of house. List all you see.

Room: _____

Words

_____

_____

_____

_____

_____

_____

Room: _____

Words

_____

_____

_____

_____

_____

_____

Room: _____

Words

_____

_____

_____

_____

_____

Room: _____

Words

_____

_____

_____

_____

_____

Questions and Answers

Your coach would like you to think about your topic by answering these questions. Think of it as interviewing yourself!

1. What colors are on the outside of your house? Do you like them? What color would you make

   _____

   _____

2. What is your house made of? Bricks? Wood? Logs? _____

   _____

3. Are there plants or big trees around the outside of your house? _____

   _____

4. How many floors are there in your house or in the building where you live? _____

5. How many windows are there in your house? How many sinks? _____

   _____

6. Do you have wallpaper, paint or paneling in your house?_____

   _____

7. Which room is the largest? The smallest?_____

   _____

8. Which room do you like the best? Why? _____

   _____

9. Where do you spend the most time in your house? _____

   _____

10. is there one room that you are almost never in? Why not? _____

    _____

Poetry

te about some of your favorite places and what you do there.

Our _____ is where we _____ ,
              (place)   (what you do)

_____ in my house.
       (repeat last word)

e is an example:

Our shower is where we get clean,
Clean in my house.
Our laundry room is where we wash the dog,
Wash the dog in my house.
Our kitchen is where we do our homework,
Homework in my house.
Get clean, wash the dog and do our homework in my house.

d with a list of all the action words.

ır _____ is where we _____ ,

_____ in my house .

ır _____ is where we _____ ,

_____ in my house .

ır _____ is where we _____ ,

_____ in my house .

ır _____ is where we _____ ,

_____ in my house .

_____ and _____ and _____ and

_____ and _____ in my house.

Four Square

This will help organize your thoughts for writing to explain why your home is special. Think of it as map for your words and ideas so they don't get lost on the way from your head to the paper! In each of the squares, write words or phrases that go with the main idea of each box. Save your se tence writing for later. Ready? Let's go!

2. One reason: _____

_____

Detail about the reason:

_____

_____

3. Another reason: _____

_____

Detail about the reason:

_____

_____

Use this sentence, or write your own beginning.

1. My home is special.

4. Another reason: _____

_____

Detail about the reason:

_____

_____

5. Now for your ending. How do you feel about your house?

_____

_____

_____

_____

A Word from Your Coach

The words in your four square will now form sentences for your writing, page 32.

Look at your four square and go to the middle box, #1. This will be the sentence that will start your writing. Go to your paper and start writing on the top line. Write a sentence with the words in this box.

Next, look at the #2 box. Make up sentences with the words in that box and write them on your paper. Make sure your writing is neat so your words can be read easily.

Go to the #3 box. Make up sentences with the words in that box. Do your sentences begin in different ways or do they begin with the same words (boring)? Write these sentences on your paper.

Go to the #4 box. Make up sentences with the words in that box. Do you use interesting and exciting words? Add these sentences to your paper.

Last, go to the #5 box. Choose an ending and write it down! If you haven't thought of a title, you might want to think of one. Add it at the top of your paper, above your writing. Now you're done!

Do the best you can!

Section 4:
Relatives Far Away

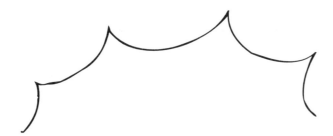

Do you ever travel to visit family far away?
Sometimes people live oceans apart
from the people they love.
We are going to draw, think and write about relatives
that we may not get to see as much as we would like to.

Recommended reading for this project:
The Relatives Came by Cynthia Rylant (Atheneum/Richard Jackson Books, 2001)

Name _____

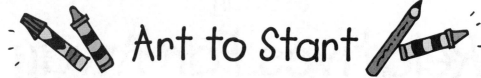 Art to Start

Before you start writing, you have pictures in your head that come first. Let's start with those pictures! Get busy with your markers, colored pencils and crayons. Think about your writing while you are drawing.

Draw a relative who lives far away from you.

Draw the way you travel to visit that person.

Draw something special that you do when you visit that person.

Word Parade

important to have words, and lots of them, parading in front of you before you start to write.
n you can pick them out when you need them. Let's start the parade by listing some words that
already in your head. Don't worry about spelling. You can fix that later. Use your mind to go on
maginary trip to your faraway relative's house. List all the things you see on your trip, when you
there and on the way home.

On the trip	Visiting	Going home
Words	Words	Words

Questions and Answers

Your coach would like you to think about your topic by answering these questions. Think of it as interviewing yourself!

1. What relatives live far away from you? _____

   _____

2. Where do they live? _____

   _____

3. How long does it take to get there? _____

   _____

4. How do you usually go there? _____

   _____

5. When was the last time you visited those relatives? _____

   _____

6. What did you do during your visit? _____

   _____

7. What can you remember about the house where the relatives live? _____

   _____

8. What do you like best about visiting these relatives? _____

   _____

9. Do these relatives sometimes come and visit you? When was the last time? _____

   _____

Poetry

te about a faraway relative and about visiting their house.

me and where he or she lives

_____ , _____

o words to describe the relative

_____ , _____

w you travel there and how long it takes

_____ , _____

ree things you do there

_____ , _____ , _____

at you like about visiting there

_____ !

re is an example:

Grandma and Grandpa, New York
Fun, playful
Airplane trip, three hours long
Eating, coloring, snuggling
I can stay up late!

Four Square

This will help organize your thoughts for writing a story about a time you went to visit relatives. Think of it as a map for your words and ideas so they don't get lost on the way from your head to the paper! In each of the squares, write words or phrases that go with the main idea of each box. Save your sentence writing for later. Ready? Let's go!

2. How you traveled there:

_____

Detail about the trip:

_____

_____

3. Describe your relative. _____

_____

How did the relative greet you?

_____

_____

Use this sentence, or write your own beginning.

1. Who you went to visit:

_____

When you went to visit:

_____

4. One thing you did at the relative's

house: _____

Detail about what you did:

_____

_____

5. Now for your ending. How did you like your trip?

_____

_____

_____

A Word from Your Coach

The words in your four square will now form sentences for your writing, page 40.

Look at your four square and go to the middle box, #1. This will be the sentence that will start your writing. Go to your paper and start writing on the top line. Write a sentence with the words in this box.

Next, look at the #2 box. Make up sentences with the words in that box and write them on your paper. Make sure your writing is neat so your words can be read easily.

Go to the #3 box. Make up sentences with the words in that box. Do your sentences begin in different ways or do they begin with the same words (boring)? Write these sentences on your paper.

Go to the #4 box. Make up sentences with the words in that box. Do you use interesting and exciting words? Add these sentences to your paper.

Last, go to the #5 box. Choose an ending and write it down! If you haven't thought of a title, you might want to think of one. Add it at the top of your paper, above your writing. Now you're done!

Ready-Set-Go!

Birthday Celebrations

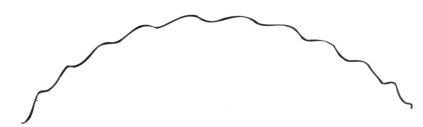

Birthdays are special times for many families.
They are a time for getting together and having fun.
Let's draw, think and write about the
celebrations in your family.

Recommended reading for this project:
It's a Monster Party! by Tasha Pym and Charles Fuge (Sterling Publishing, 2003)

Name _____

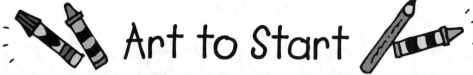 

Art to Start

Before you start writing, you have pictures in your head that come first. Let's start with those pictures! Get busy with your markers, colored pencils and crayons. Think about your writing while you are drawing.

Draw the best birthday cake
you ever remember.

Draw some of the people who help
you celebrate your birthday.

Draw something from the best birthday party you could ever have.

Word Parade

important to have words, and lots of them, parading in front of you before you start to write. en you can pick them out when you need them. Let's start the parade by listing some words that already in your head. Don't worry about spelling. You can fix that later. If you are going to plan perfect birthday party, you need to start with a list. List all the things you need to make a fect party.

Questions and Answers

Your coach would like you to think about your topic by answering these questions. Think of it as interviewing yourself!

1. How did you celebrate your last birthday? _____

   _____

2. How many people joined in the celebration? _____

3. What special treats or foods did you enjoy? _____

   _____

4. Are there certain birthdays that have special celebrations in your family? What kind?

   _____

   _____

5. What are some of the best birthday gifts you have ever given? What made them so good?

   _____

   _____

6. What are some of the best birthday gifts you have ever received? Why are they the best?

   _____

   _____

7. Do you have separate parties for friends and for family? _____

   _____

8. What wish do you have for your next birthday? _____

   _____

Poetry

u are going to write a poem about a loud, crazy birthday party. It will feel like the party is going right around you!

noise at the party
hat the noise was
peat as many times as you like

re is an example:

Ding dong
My best friend is here
Whoopee
Another guest
Pop
There goes a balloon

e as many lines as you need to describe the perfect birthday party.

_____

_____

_____

_____

_____

_____

_____

_____

_____

_____

Four Square

This will help organize your thoughts for writing to describe your last great party. Think of it as a map for your words and ideas so they don't get lost on the way from your head to the paper! In each of the squares, write words or phrases that go with the main idea of each box. Save your sentence writing for later. Ready? Let's go!

2. One thing you did at the party:

_____

Detail about what you did:

_____

_____

3. One thing you ate at the party:

_____

Detail about the food:

_____

_____

Use this sentence, or write your own beginning.

1. Who had the party?

_____

Where was the party?

_____

4. One game you played at the party:

_____

Detail about the game:

_____

_____

5. Now for your ending. Why was this the best party?

_____

_____

_____

_____

A Word from Your Coach

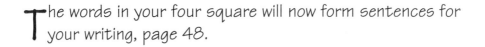

The words in your four square will now form sentences for your writing, page 48.

Look at your four square and go to the middle box, #1. This will be the sentence that will start your writing. Go to your paper and start writing on the top line. Write a sentence with the words in this box.

Next, look at the #2 box. Make up sentences with the words in that box and write them on your paper. Make sure your writing is neat so your words can be read easily.

Go to the #3 box. Make up sentences with the words in that box. Do your sentences begin in different ways or do they begin with the same words (boring)? Write these sentences on your paper.

Go to the #4 box. Make up sentences with the words in that box. Do you use interesting and exciting words? Add these sentences to your paper.

Last, go to the #5 box. Choose an ending and write it down! If you haven't thought of a title, you might want to think of one. Add it at the top of your paper, above your writing. Now you're done!

Give your best effort!

Section 6:
Holidays

Many families have special traditions for the holidays.
How does your family celebrate?
We will write about the special times you share.

Recommended reading for this project:
The Polar Express by Chris Van Allsburg (Houghton Mifflin, 1985)

Name _____

 # Art to Start

Before you start writing, you have pictures in your head that come first. Let's start with those pictures! Get busy with your markers, colored pencils and crayons. Think about your writing while you are drawing.

Draw a scene from a winter holiday.	Draw a scene from a summer holiday.

Draw a scene from a spring holiday.	Draw a scene from an autumn holiday.

50

Word Parade

important to have words, and lots of them, parading in front of you before you start to write.
n you can pick them out when you need them. Let's start the parade by listing some words that
already in your head. Don't worry about spelling. You can fix that later. Think about some of
r favorite holidays. Then write the words that come to mind when you think about them.

Holiday _____

Words

_____

_____

_____

_____

Holiday _____

Words

_____

_____

_____

_____

Holiday _____

Words

_____

_____

_____

_____

Holiday _____

Words

_____

_____

_____

_____

Name _____

Questions and Answers

Your coach would like you to think about your topic by answering these questions. Think of it as interviewing yourself!

1. What holidays does your family celebrate? _____

_____

2. Do you celebrate them in your house or someplace else? Where? _____

_____

3. Are there special foods? What are they? _____

_____

4. What special things does your family do to prepare your house for the holiday? _____

_____

_____

5. Are there special things that the grown-ups do? The kids? What are they? _____

_____

_____

6. Sometimes families get specially dressed up for a holiday. Does your family? What do you wear?

_____

7. What is your favorite family holiday celebration? Why is it your favorite? _____

_____

8. On what holidays does your family exchange presents? _____

_____

Poetry

poem will help you write about your favorite holiday. Just follow the form.

me of the holiday
o things that go with the holiday
ound word that goes with the holiday
e thing that you do on the holiday
e season of the holiday
mething special about the holiday

e is an example:

Hanukkah
Dreidles, candles
The crackle of the potato pancakes in the pan
Playing the dreidel game with my sisters
Early winter
Eight nights long!

v you try it.

_____

_____

_____

_____

_____

_____

Four Square

This will help organize your thoughts for writing to explain why a particular holiday is your favorit.
Think of it as a map for your words and ideas so they don't get lost on the way from your head t
the paper! In each of the squares, write words or phrases that go with the main idea of each bo;
Save your sentence writing for later. Ready? Let's go!

2. One reason it is your favorite:

_____

Detail about the reason:

_____

_____

3. Another reason: _____

_____

Detail about the reason:

_____

_____

Use this sentence, or write your own beginning.

1. _____

is my favorite holiday.

4. Another reason: _____

_____

Detail about the reason:

_____

_____

5. Now for your ending. How do you feel
on the holiday?

_____

_____

_____

_____

A Word from Your Coach

The words in your four square will now form sentences for your writing, page 56.

Look at your four square and go to the middle box, #1. This will be the sentence that will start your writing. Go to your paper and start writing on the top line. Write a sentence with the words in this box.

Next, look at the #2 box. Make up sentences with the words in that box and write them on your paper. Make sure your writing is neat so your words can be read easily.

Go to the #3 box. Make up sentences with the words in that box. Do your sentences begin in different ways or do they begin with the same words (boring)? Write these sentences on your paper.

Go to the #4 box. Make up sentences with the words in that box. Do you use interesting and exciting words? Add these sentences to your paper.

Last, go to the #5 box. Choose an ending and write it down! If you haven't thought of a title, you might want to think of one. Add it at the top of your paper, above your writing. Now you're done!

This sounds terrific!

Section 7:
Hanging out at Home

Some of the best times as a family
are spent doing almost nothing!
Think about lazy, rainy days at home
or fun at the park or in the yard.
These can be really special family times.

Recommended reading for this project:
Jumanji by Chris Van Allsburg (Houghton Miffin, 1981)
Edward and the Pirates by David McPhail (Little, Brown, 1997)
Tar Beach by Faith Ringgold (Dragonfly Books, 1996)

Name _____

 # Art to Start

Before you start writing, you have pictures in your head that come first. Let's start with those pictures! Get busy with your markers, colored pencils and crayons. Think about your writing while you are drawing.

> Draw one thing that your family
> does at home for fun.

> Draw one place that your
> family has fun at home.

> Draw one thing that your family
> does on rainy days.

> Draw one thing that your family
> does in your yard or at the park.

Word Parade

mportant to have words, and lots of them, parading in front of you before you start to write.
you can pick them out when you need them. Let's start the parade by listing some words that
already in your head. Don't worry about spelling. You can fix that later.

a walk inside your house and make a list of all the things that your family could do to have fun
ther. Don't forget the kitchen. There is a lot there, too!

Questions and Answers

Your coach would like you to think about your topic by answering these questions. Think of it as interviewing yourself!

1. When does your family get to just hang around together? _____

2. Is there a special activity or game you play sometimes? _____

   _____

3. Do the grown-ups play, or just kids? _____

   _____

4. Are there special things you do on rainy days? Snowy days? _____

   _____

5. Does your family do special projects together? _____

   _____

6. What are some special treats your family has together? _____

   _____

7. On a nice day, what can you and your family play outside? _____

   _____

   _____

8. Are there some times when the grown-ups in your family act like kids? When? What do they

   _____

   _____

9. What is the most fun you have had with your family, without even leaving your house?

   _____

   _____

Poetry

poem will help you write about things that are boring and things that are not.

oring day is _____

a fun day is when we _____

these two sentences as many times as you like.
with a wish about the day you want to have.

e is an example:

A boring day is cleaning
But a fun day is playing cards.
A boring day is a rainy day
But a fun day is watching movies.
I wish for a day with my family!

_____
_____
_____
_____
_____
_____
_____
_____
_____
_____
_____

Four Square

This will help organize your thoughts for writing to explain what you and your family do to have fun. Think of it as a map for your words and ideas so they don't get lost on the way from your head to the paper! In each of the squares, write words or phrases that go with the main idea of each box. Save your sentence writing for later. Ready? Let's go!

2. One thing that you do for fun:

_____

Detail about the reason:

_____

_____

3. One thing that you do for fun:

_____

A reason why you like it:

_____

_____

Use this sentence, or write your own beginning.

1. My family can have fun when we just hang out.

4. One thing that you do for fun:

_____

A reason why you like it:

_____

_____

5. Now for your ending. The best part about hanging around with your family:

_____

_____

_____

_____

A Word from Your Coach

The words in your four square will now form sentences for your writing, page 64.

Look at your four square and go to the middle box, #1. This will be the sentence that will start your writing. Go to your paper and start writing on the top line. Write a sentence with the words in this box.

Next, look at the #2 box. Make up sentences with the words in that box and write them on your paper. Make sure your writing is neat so your words can be read easily.

Go to the #3 box. Make up sentences with the words in that box. Do your sentences begin in different ways or do they begin with the same words (boring)? Write these sentences on your paper.

Go to the #4 box. Make up sentences with the words in that box. Do you use interesting and exciting words? Add these sentences to your paper.

Last, go to the #5 box. Choose an ending and write it down! If you haven't thought of a title, you might want to think of one. Add it at the top of your paper, above your writing. Now you're done!

I'm here if you need me!

My Favorite Time with Someone Special

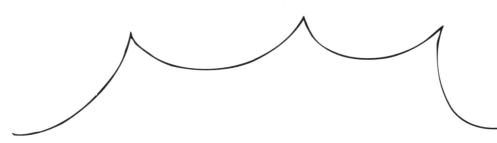

It is great to have so many special people in your life.
Spending time with them can be fun if you
go somewhere exciting or just stay home.

Recommended reading for this project:

Tell Me One Thing, Dad by Tom Pow and Ian Andrew (Candlewick Press, 2004)
Abuela by Arthur Dorros and Elisa Kleven (Puffin Books, 1997)

Name _____

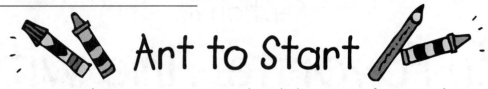 # Art to Start

Before you start writing, you have pictures in your head that come first. Let's start with those pictures! Get busy with your markers, colored pencils and crayons. Think about your writing while you are drawing.

Draw a person who shared a special time with you.	Draw how you felt with that person.

Draw one thing that you did together.

Word Parade

important to have words, and lots of them, parading in front of you before you start to write.
n you can pick them out when you need them. Let's start the parade by listing some words that
already in your head. Don't worry about spelling. You can fix that later. Think about the special
e you had together. Make a list of everything you did and everything you saw.

What you did: _____

Words

_____   _____

_____   _____

_____   _____

_____   _____

What you saw: _____

Words

_____   _____

_____   _____

_____   _____

_____   _____

Name _____

Questions and Answers

Your coach would like you to think about your topic by answering these questions. Think of it as interviewing yourself!

1. Can you think of a time when you did something extra special? What was it? _____

_____

2. Who shared your special time with you? _____

_____

3. What did that person do to help make your time together so special? _____

_____

4. When was the special time you had together?_____

_____

5. Did you go someplace? Where?_____

_____

6. Why was this time so special for you? _____

_____

_____

7. Did you ever get to do this thing again? Or with someone else? _____

_____

8. Did your special time together cost money? _____

_____

9. Could this special time happen with anyone else, or only with that person?_____

_____

Poetry

are ready to write about the time that you had together.

ree things you saw
e person's name
o things you did
en you had the special day
o things you saw
e person's name
e thing you did (the best thing you did together)

e is an example:

Ice cream, sprinkles, crowds of people
My sister Nat
Shopping and talking
A cold December day
A beautiful shirt, a new CD
Natalie
Spending time together

_____
_____
_____
_____
_____
_____
_____
_____
_____
_____
_____

Four Square

This will help organize your thoughts for writing to describe a special day you had with a friend or relative. Think of it as a map for your words and ideas so they don't get lost on the way from your head to the paper! In each of the squares, write words or phrases that go with the main idea of each box. Save your sentence writing for later. Ready? Let's go!

2. One thing you did together: _____

_____

Detail about what you did:

_____

_____

3. Something that you saw together:

_____

Detail about what you saw:

_____

_____

Use this sentence, or write your own beginning.

1. I shared a special day with

_____

4. The best part about being together:

_____

Why it was the best:

_____

_____

5. Now for your ending. How you felt during your time together:

_____

_____

_____

A Word from Your Coach

The words in your four square will now form sentences for your writing, page 72.

Look at your four square and go to the middle box, #1. This will be the sentence that will start your writing. Go to your paper and start writing on the top line. Write a sentence with the words in this box.

Next, look at the #2 box. Make up sentences with the words in that box and write them on your paper. Make sure your writing is neat so your words can be read easily.

Go to the #3 box. Make up sentences with the words in that box. Do your sentences begin in different ways or do they begin with the same words (boring)? Write these sentences on your paper.

Go to the #4 box. Make up sentences with the words in that box. Do you use interesting and exciting words? Add these sentences to your paper.

Last, go to the #5 box. Choose an ending and write it down! If you haven't thought of a title, you might want to think of one. Add it at the top of your paper, above your writing. Now you're done!

Where We Like to Go

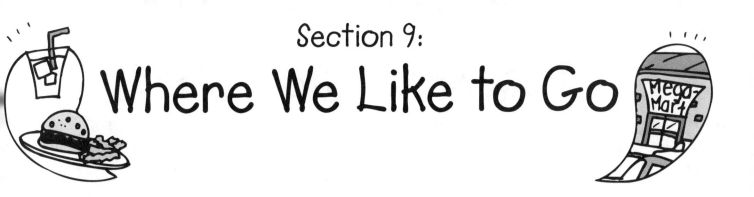

Whether it is to the store, or out to dinner at a favorite restaurant, most of us have favorite places we like to go. Going there can be special when you share the time with friends and family.

Recommended reading for this project:

Sidewalk Circus by Paul Fleischman and Kevin Hawkes (Candlewick Press, 2004)
America Is by Louise Borden (Margaret K. McElderry, 2002)

Name _____

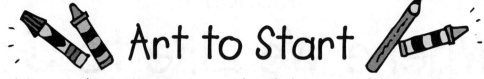 

Art to Start

Before you start writing, you have pictures in your head that come first. Let's start with those pictures! Get busy with your markers, colored pencils and crayons. Think about your writing while you are drawing.

Draw the front of the place you like to go.

Draw the inside of the place.

Draw a picture of what you like to do there.

Word Parade

important to have words, and lots of them, parading in front of you before you start to write.
n you can pick them out when you need them. Let's start the parade by listing some words that
already in your head. Don't worry about spelling. You can fix that later. Think of the places you
to go and the words that go with them.

Place_____

Words

_____

_____

_____

_____

Place_____

Words

_____

_____

_____

_____

Place_____

Words

_____

_____

_____

_____

Place_____

Words

_____

_____

_____

_____

Name _____

Questions and Answers

Your coach would like you to think about your topic by answering these questions. Think of it as interviewing yourself!

1. What is the name of the place your family likes to go to get groceries? _____

2. Do you sometimes go along? What do you do in the store? _____

_____

3. Do you sometimes get a fast-food supper from a pizza place or a burger place? What is the

name of the place? How often do you go there? _____

_____

4. Do you sometimes visit big stores to buy clothing? What are names of the stores? _____

_____

5. What are some of your favorite restaurants in town? _____

_____

6. Why do you like to go there? _____

_____

7. Do you sometimes go out just for fun, such as to the movies or a roller-skating rink? How

often? With whom? _____

_____

8. Do you go to special places with friends sometimes? Which friends? _____

_____

9. Do you go to see the doctor or dentist? What are their names? What do you think about go

there? _____

_____

Poetry

are ready to write about the places you like to go.

e thing you do
o things you see
e place that you go

this form as many times as you need to write about all the places you like to go.

e is an example:

Riding in the cart
The shiny apples and the cold ice cream
At the grocery store

_____

_____

_____

_____

_____

_____

_____

_____

_____

_____

Name _____

Four Square

This will help organize your thoughts for writing to describe a special place you like to go. Think of as a map for your words and ideas so they don't get lost on the way from your head to the pape In each of the squares, write words or phrases that go with the main idea of each box. Save your sentence writing for later. Ready? Let's go!

2. When you go there: _____

_____

Who goes with you:

_____

_____

3. Something that you do there:

_____

Tell more about what you do:

_____

Use this sentence, or write your own beginning.

1. I like to go to

_____

4. One thing that you see there:

_____

Detail about what you see:

_____

_____

5. Now for your ending. How you felt during your time at this place:

_____

_____

_____

A Word from Your Coach

The words in your four square will now form sentences for your writing, page 80.

Look at your four square and go to the middle box, #1. This will be the sentence that will start your writing. Go to your paper and start writing on the top line. Write a sentence with the words in this box.

Next, look at the #2 box. Make up sentences with the words in that box and write them on your paper. Make sure your writing is neat so your words can be read easily.

Go to the #3 box. Make up sentences with the words in that box. Do your sentences begin in different ways or do they begin with the same words (boring)? Write these sentences on your paper.

Go to the #4 box. Make up sentences with the words in that box. Do you use interesting and exciting words? Add these sentences to your paper.

Last, go to the #5 box. Choose an ending and write it down! If you haven't thought of a title, you might want to think of one. Add it at the top of your paper, above your writing. Now you're done!

Section 10:
Chow Time

This delicious subject may
make you hungry just thinking about it.
Food is nearly everywhere we go.
What are some of your favorites?
We will be thinking and writing about food.

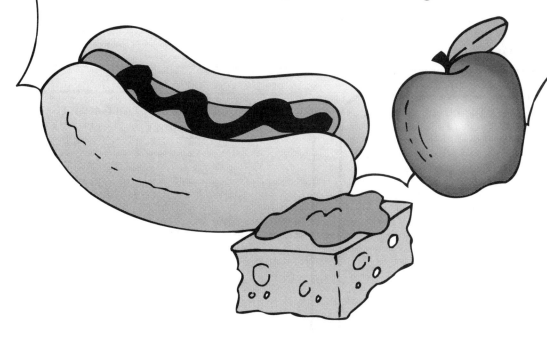

Recommended reading for this project:

Food Fight! by Carol Diggory and Doreen Gay-Kassel (Handprint Books, 2002)

Blueberries for Sal by Robert McCloskey (Puffin Books, 1976)

A Bad Case of Stripes by David Shannon (Scholastic Paperbacks, 2004)

Name _____

Art to Start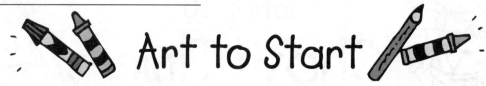

Before you start writing, you have pictures in your head that come first. Let's start with those pictures! Get busy with your markers, colored pencils and crayons. Think about your writing while you are drawing.

Draw your favorite breakfast.	Draw your favorite lunch.

Draw your favorite dinner.	Draw your favorite snack.

Word Parade

important to have words, and lots of them, parading in front of you before you start to write.
n you can pick them out when you need them. Let's start the parade by listing some words that
already in your head. Don't worry about spelling. You can fix that later. Think of all the foods
like to eat and the words that go with them.

Food _____

Words

_____

_____

_____

_____

Food _____

Words

_____

_____

_____

_____

Food _____

Words

_____

_____

_____

_____

Food _____

Words

_____

_____

_____

_____

Questions and Answers

Your coach would like you to think about your topic by answering these questions. Think of it as interviewing yourself!

1. What is your favorite thing to eat? _____

2. When do you get to have this special food? _____

_____

3. Who prepares your favorite foods for you? _____

_____

4. What is your favorite thing to have for breakfast? Lunch? Dinner? _____

_____

5. Do you have a sweet tooth? What are some of your favorite treats? _____

_____

6. Do you like special desserts? What are your favorites? _____

_____

7. Do you sometimes help to make the food at home? How do you help? _____

_____

8. Sometimes the holidays bring special foods. What are some of your favorite holiday foods?

_____

_____

9. Are there some foods your just don't want to eat? What are they? Why don't you like them?

_____

_____

Poetry

are ready to write about some foods. Just follow the pattern.

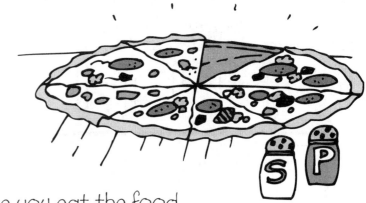

ood

oise you make when eating it

o words that tell how it tastes

e word that tells how it looks

e word that tells how it smells

e word that tells how it feels

ime when you eat the food or where you eat the food

e is an example:

Pizza

Mmmm, yum

Saucy and cheesy

Hot

Spicy

Stringy

At Joe's Pizzeria

_____

_____

_____

_____

_____

_____

_____

Four Square

This will help organize your thoughts for writing to describe a special food you like to eat. Think o
as a map for your words and ideas so they don't get lost on the way from your head to the pape
In each of the squares, write words or phrases that go with the main idea of each box. Save your
sentence writing for later. Ready? Let's go!

2. When you eat it: _____

_____

Tell more about when:

_____

_____

3. How you eat it: _____

_____

Tell more about how:

_____

_____

Use this sentence, or write your own beginning.

1. I love to eat

_____

4. What you eat with it: _____

_____

Detail about what you eat with it:

_____

_____

5. Now for your ending. Why do you like
this food so much?

_____

_____

_____

A Word from Your Coach

The words in your four square will now form sentences for your writing, page 88.

Look at your four square and go to the middle box, #1. This will be the sentence that will start your writing. Go to your paper and start writing on the top line. Write a sentence with the words in this box.

Next, look at the #2 box. Make up sentences with the words in that box and write them on your paper. Make sure your writing is neat so your words can be read easily.

Go to the #3 box. Make up sentences with the words in that box. Do your sentences begin in different ways or do they begin with the same words (boring)? Write these sentences on your paper.

Go to the #4 box. Make up sentences with the words in that box. Do you use interesting and exciting words? Add these sentences to your paper.

Last, go to the #5 box. Choose an ending and write it down! If you haven't thought of a title, you might want to think of one. Add it at the top of your paper, above your writing. Now you're done!

Go for it!

Section 11:
After-School Fun

What's more fun than being done with school for the day?
Think about what you *do after school* that you enjoy . . .
Ready? Here we go!

Recommended reading for this project:
The Snowy Day by Ezra Jack Keats (Viking Books, 1976)
We're Going on a Bear Hunt by Michael Rosen (Aladdin paper back, 2003)

Name _____

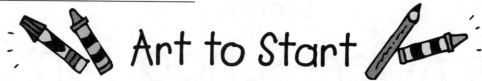

Art to Start

Before you start writing, you have pictures in your head that come first. Let's start with those pictures! Get busy with your markers, colored pencils and crayons. Think about your writing while you are drawing.

Draw something that you like to do after school.	Draw the place where you do this activity.
Draw any equipment, material or any special things that you need to do this special activity.	Draw the people you do this activity with.

Word Parade

important to have words, and lots of them, parading in front of you before you start to write.
n you can pick them out when you need them. Let's start the parade by listing some words that
already in your head. Don't worry about spelling. You can fix that later.

List all the activities you like doing after school.	List all the things you use to enjoy your after-school activities.
List how you feel when you're doing your after-school activities.	List all the people that are with you when you do these activities.

Name _____

Questions and Answers

Your coach would like you to think about your topic by answering these questions. Think of it as interviewing yourself!

1. What do you like to do after school? _____

2. Is this activity sports related or does it involve a particular talent like playing an instrument

   _____

3. How many activities do you participate in after school? Name them. _____

   _____

4. Do you have a favorite? Why is this one your favorite? _____

   _____

5. What kind of equipment or materials do you need for this activity? Describe them._____

   _____

   _____

6. Is there a special location where this activity takes place? Tell about it. _____

   _____

7. Who are the friends that share this activity with you? Is there someone who is your favorite?

   Tell why. _____

   _____

8. Tell something about the grown-up who supervises you for this activity. _____

   _____

9. What is it about this activity that you love so much?_____

   _____

   _____

Poetry

ting isn't always about a story. Poems are a great way of getting your feelings down in a shorter
. Poems are fun and remember, they don't always have to rhyme! In fact, this one doesn't rhyme
ss you want it to.

me the activity

scribe the place where you do this activity

 verb + detail

 verb + detail

 verb + detail

 verb + detail

ite how you feel about the activity

e is an example:

Soccer practice
On a muddy field,
Sliding in the mud,
Sprinting down field,
Heading a slick ball,
Crashing into muddy players,
Nothing better than playing soccer after a thunderstorm

_____

_____

_____

_____

_____

_____

_____

Four Square

This will help organize your thoughts for writing to describe the best way to spend time after sch
Think of it as a map for your words and ideas so they don't get lost on the way from your head t.
the paper! In each of the squares, write words or phrases that go with the main idea of each box
Save your sentence writing for later. Ready? Let's go!

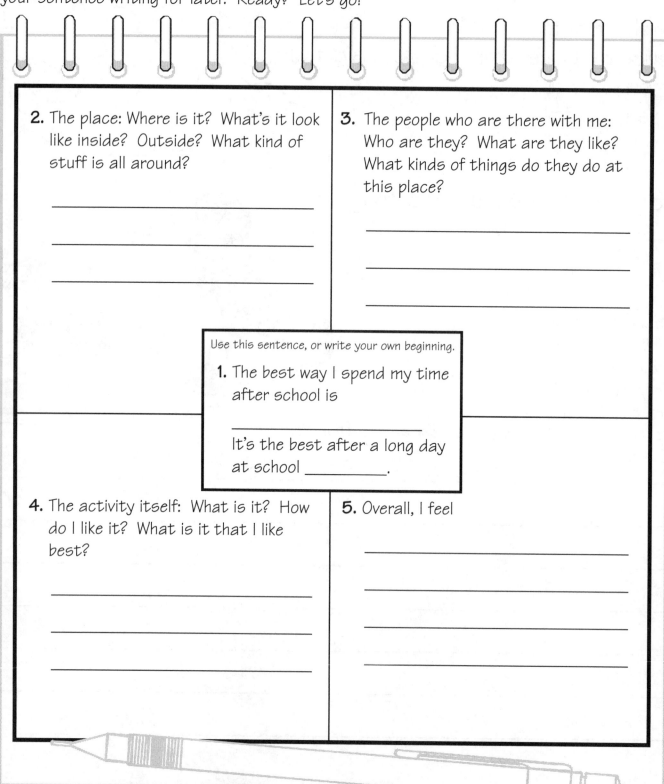

2. The place: Where is it? What's it look like inside? Outside? What kind of stuff is all around?

_____

_____

_____

3. The people who are there with me: Who are they? What are they like? What kinds of things do they do at this place?

_____

_____

_____

Use this sentence, or write your own beginning.

1. The best way I spend my time after school is

_____

It's the best after a long day at school _____.

4. The activity itself: What is it? How do I like it? What is it that I like best?

_____

_____

_____

5. Overall, I feel

_____

_____

_____

A Word from Your Coach

The words in your four square will now form sentences for your writing, page 95.

Look at your four square and go to the middle box, #1. This will be the sentence that will start your writing. Go to your paper and start writing on the top line. Write a sentence with the words in this box.

Next, look at the #2 box. Make up sentences with the words in that box and write them on your paper. Make sure your writing is neat so your words can be read easily.

Go to the #3 box. Make up sentences with the words in that box. Do your sentences begin in different ways or do they begin with the same words (boring)? Write these sentences on your paper.

Go to the #4 box. Make up sentences with the words in that box. Do you use interesting and exciting words? Add these sentences to your paper.

Last, go to the #5 box. Choose an ending and write it down! If you haven't thought of a title, you might want to think of one. Add it at the top of your paper, above your writing. Now you're done!

I believe in YOU!

96

Section 12:
My Neighborhood

Thinking about where we live
helps us to know who we are!
Look around you.
What *do* you see?
Are you ready to write about it?
Let's begin!

Recommended reading for this project:
The House Across the Street by Jules Feiffer (Michael D. Capua Books, 2002)

Name _____

 Art to Start

Before you start writing, you have pictures in your head that come first. Let's start with those pictures! Get busy with your markers, colored pencils and crayons. Think about your writing while you are drawing.

Draw a picture of what you see when you look out your bedroom window.

Draw a picture of the house that is closest to yours.

Draw a picture of one of your neighbors.

Draw a picture of the most interesting thing in your neighborhood.

Word Parade

important to have words, and lots of them, parading in front of you before you start to write.
you can pick them out when you need them. Let's start the parade by listing some words that
already in your head. Don't worry about spelling. You can fix that later.

List all the things that are on either side of your house.	List all the words that describe your neighborhood.
_____	_____
_____	_____
_____	_____
_____	_____
List all the special things that are in your neighborhood.	**List all the things you would add to your neighborhood to make it more interesting.**
_____	_____
_____	_____
_____	_____
_____	_____

Name _____

Questions and Answers

Your coach would like you to think about your topic by answering these questions. Think of it as interviewing yourself!

1. How long have you lived in your neighborhood? _____

2. Do you have any friends in your neighborhood? If yes, who are they?_____
   _____

3. What do you like best about your neighborhood? _____
   _____

4. What don't you like about your neighborhood? _____
   _____

5. Does your neighborhood have a name? What is it? If you could rename your neighborhood, wh
   would its new name be? Why?_____
   _____

6. If you could change anything about your neighborhood, what would it be? Why? _____
   _____

7. Are there any special places (stores, restaurants, parks) in your neighborhood? What are th
   What makes them special? _____
   _____

8. If you could create the perfect neighborhood, what would it be like?_____
   _____

9. If you could add one thing to your neighborhood, what would it be? Why would you add that o
   thing?_____
   _____

Poetry

...ing isn't always about a story. Poems are a great way of getting your feelings down in a shorter ... Don't panic! Poems are fun and remember they don't always have to rhyme! In fact, this one ...sn't rhyme unless you want it to.

...neighborhood
...o great because

_____

_____

(use a describing word here)

...d _____

(use a describing word here)

...if I could I would
...ange my neighborhood

_____

_____

...would make my neighborhood
...n more fun!

Here is an example:

My neighborhood
Is so great because
There's the biggest sycamore tree
Right at the corner of our street.

It's shady
And so green!

But if I could I would
Change my neighborhood
By adding a giant tree
House in that sycamore tree.

It would make my neighborhood
Even more fun!

WOW!

Name _____

Four Square

This will help organize your thoughts for writing to describe your neighborhood. Think of it as a m
for your words and ideas so they don't get lost on the way from your head to the paper! In each
the squares, write words or phrases that go with the main idea of each box. Save your sentence
writing for later. Ready? Let's go!

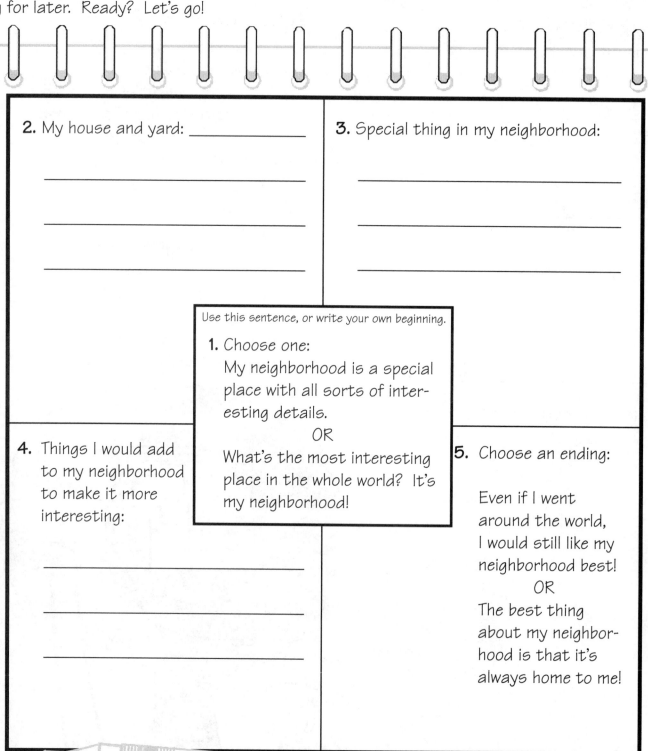

2. My house and yard: _____

_____

_____

_____

3. Special thing in my neighborhood:

_____

_____

_____

Use this sentence, or write your own beginning.

1. Choose one:
My neighborhood is a special place with all sorts of interesting details.
        OR
What's the most interesting place in the whole world? It's my neighborhood!

4. Things I would add to my neighborhood to make it more interesting:

_____

_____

_____

5. Choose an ending:

Even if I went around the world, I would still like my neighborhood best!
        OR
The best thing about my neighborhood is that it's always home to me!

A Word from Your Coach

The words in your four square will now form sentences for your writing, page 104.

Look at your four square and go to the middle box, #1. This will be the sentence that will start your writing. Go to your paper and start writing on the top line. Write a sentence with the words in this box.

Next, look at the #2 box. Make up sentences with the words in that box and write them on your paper. Make sure your writing is neat so your words can be read easily.

Go to the #3 box. Make up sentences with the words in that box. Do your sentences begin in different ways or do they begin with the same words (boring)? Write these sentences on your paper.

Go to the #4 box. Make up sentences with the words in that box. Do you use interesting and exciting words? Add these sentences to your paper.

Last, go to the #5 box. Choose an ending and write it down! If you haven't thought of a title, you might want to think of one. Add it at the top of your paper, above your writing. Now you're done!

Section 13:
Treats

Everyone loves a treat!
Some people like sweet treats while others like salty ones.
Some people like treats that stick to the
roof of their mouths! So now it's time to think
of all the treats you like and write about them.
Ready? Here we go!

Recommended reading for this project:
Bread and Jam for Frances by Russell Hoban (HarperCollins, 1993)

Name _____

Art to Start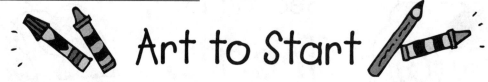

Before you start writing, you have pictures in your head that come first. Let's start with those pictures! Get busy with your markers, colored pencils and crayons. Think about your writing while you are drawing.

Draw your favorite after-school treat.

Draw your favorite movie snack.

Draw your favorite Saturday night treat.

Draw your favorite treat when you're playing with your friends.

Word Parade

important to have words, and lots of them, parading in front of you before you start to write. you can pick them out when you need them. Let's start the parade by listing some words that already in your head. Don't worry about spelling. You can fix that later.

Write the names of your favorite treats. _____ _____ _____ _____	**Choose one treat and write words that tell what it's like in your mouth.** *Example: Popcorn* *Crunchy, salty, buttery* _____ _____ _____ _____
Choose another treat and write words that tell how it tastes. _____ _____ _____ _____	**Write that words that make a sound in your mouth whenever you eat your treats.** *Example: slurp, crunch, smack* _____ _____ _____ _____

Name _____

Questions and Answers

Your coach would like you to think about your topic by answering these questions. Think of it as interviewing yourself!

1. What is your favorite after-school snack? _____

2. Why is this your favorite? _____

   _____

3. What kind of sound does it make in your mouth when you're eating it? _____

   _____

4. What's your favorite movie treat? _____

5. Why do you like eating this treat while you're at the movies? _____

   _____

6. What kind of sound does it make in your mouth when you're eating it? _____

   _____

7. If a famous person came to visit you and wanted a snack, what treat would you offer? Why?

   _____

   _____

8. Do you think you could invent a new snack? What would it look like? What would it taste like?

   How would it sound? What would you call it? _____

   _____

   _____

Poetry

...ing isn't always about a story. Poems are a great way of getting your feelings down in a shorter ... Don't panic! Poems are fun and remember, they don't always have to rhyme! In fact, this one ...n't rhyme unless you want it to.

...his out!

...when you eat this treat.
...n list words to describe this treat.
...t, tell how you feel about it.

_____

_____

_____

_____

_____

_____

_____

_____

_____

_____

Here is an example:

At the movies, I gobble down popcorn!
Yummy
Buttery
Salty
Crunchy
Tasty
Popcorn

I could eat a ton!

Name _____

Four Square

This will help organize your thoughts for writing to describe your favorite treat. Think of it as a n
for your words and ideas so they don't get lost on the way from your head to the paper! In each
the squares, write words or phrases that go with the main idea of each box. Save your sentence
writing for later. Ready? Let's go!

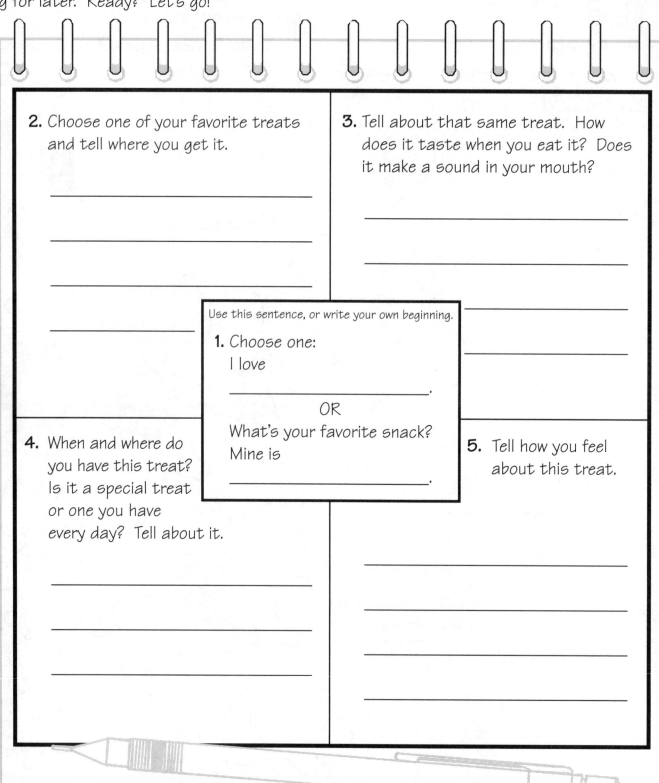

2. Choose one of your favorite treats and tell where you get it.

_____

_____

_____

3. Tell about that same treat. How does it taste when you eat it? Does it make a sound in your mouth?

_____

_____

_____

Use this sentence, or write your own beginning.

1. Choose one:
I love

_____.

OR

What's your favorite snack?
Mine is

_____.

4. When and where do you have this treat? Is it a special treat or one you have every day? Tell about it.

_____

_____

_____

5. Tell how you feel about this treat.

_____

_____

_____

A Word from Your Coach

The words in your four square will now form sentences for your writing, page 112.

Look at your four square and go to the middle box, #1. This will be the sentence that will start your writing. Go to your paper and start writing on the top line. Write a sentence with the words in this box.

Next, look at the #2 box. Make up sentences with the words in that box and write them on your paper. Make sure your writing is neat so your words can be read easily.

Go to the #3 box. Make up sentences with the words in that box. Do your sentences begin in different ways or do they begin with the same words (boring)? Write these sentences on your paper.

Go to the #4 box. Make up sentences with the words in that box. Do you use interesting and exciting words? Add these sentences to your paper.

Last, go to the #5 box. Choose an ending and write it down! If you haven't thought of a title, you might want to think of one. Add it at the top of your paper, above your writing. Now you're done!

You'll do an awesome job!

PURCHASING FROM SMALL WOMEN–OWNED SUPPLIERS

by

Carol L. Ketchum

Susan M. Olson

Alan E. Campbell

Gabrielle Aguayo

**Center for Advanced Purchasing Studies/
National Association of Purchasing Management**

PURCHASING FROM SMALL WOMEN-OWNED SUPPLIERS

by

Carol L. Ketchum

Susan M. Olson

Alan E. Campbell

Gabrielle Aguayo

ACKNOWLEDGMENTS •

The Center for Advanced Purchasing Studies and the authors wish to thank the participants from the 180 firms who provided the data on which this research report is based. We are also grateful for the project's major support from U S WEST Business Resources, Inc., Northern Telecom Inc., and the ARCO Foundation.

A special thanks goes to Gabrielle Aguayo, a loaned executive from U S WEST Business Resources, Inc., for her assistance in the interview and survey phases of the study.

We would also like to thank the CAPS Secretaries, Wendy Richards and J. Michelle Gomez, for their clerical assistance, as well as Richard Boyle, Assistant Director, and Linda Stanley, Graduate Research Associate, for their administrative support.

Finally, the industry/research/advisory committee for this study reviewed the manuscript and helped strengthen its analysis and presentation. Special thanks are due to:

1. Don Zuber, Pacific Bell
2. Liz Kahnk, TRY US, National Minority Business Directories
3. Angela Dermyer, Union Pacific Railroad
4. Alvin Williams, University of Southern Mississippi
5. William Bales, (formerly) Union Pacific Railroad

Of course, complete responsibility for the final study rests with the authors of this report.

ISBN: 0-945968-05-1

CONTENTS •

EXHIBITS, TABLES, FIGURES, AND APPENDICES •

PREFACE •

This report outlines many of the impediments Women Business Enterprises (WBEs) and Corporate Purchasing Personnel (CPPs) face when the two parties attempt to conduct business with each other. Several activities are suggested to overcome the impediments faced by both parties.

The study should not be viewed as a definitive answer to the hindrances WBEs and CPPs face when transacting business. Rather, it is meant to further an understanding of the issues involved and encourage further research into the problems that exist.

SUMMARY AND IMPLICATIONS OF THE STUDY •

Corporate Purchasing Personnel (CPP) have developed Women Business Enterprise (WBE) purchasing programs partly in response to pressures applied by women and minority groups, and by government. Adding new and capable suppliers to the vendor base is another reason why CPPs have established WBE programs.

However, certain impediments exist when WBEs and CPPs conduct business. This conclusion is based on a 1990 study sponsored by the National Association of Purchasing Management's and Arizona State University's Center for Advanced Purchasing Studies (CAPS). Eight variables are suggested to explain these impediments. When the costs associated with these variables become excessive, impediments form that discourage business transactions. Exhibit 1 lists the eight variables and provides a brief definition of each.

EXHIBIT 1
DEFINITIONS OF THE IMPEDIMENT VARIABLES

Bounded Rationality (Complexity):	The costs of dealing with large bureaucracies, inconsistent procedures, and large quantities of information.
Opportunism:	The costs of unprincipled or unscrupulous behavior.
Few Firms:	The costs of searching for the small number of vendors available.
Business Uncertainty:	The costs of incorrectly assessing another party's ability to perform and survive.
Production Uncertainty:	The costs of producing quality output efficiently and effectively.
Impacted Information:	The cost to one party when the other in a negotiation has more information.
Atmosphere:	The personal costs of conducting business in a tense environment.
Resource Dependence:	The extent to which one transacting party relies on the contract for its business.

The major conclusions of this study are:

1. WBEs report that having too little capital for efficient operation or undercapitalization of their businesses is the largest single impediment to conducting business successfully. This conclusion is in sharp contrast to the findings of a similar study concerning Minority Business Enterprises (MBEs). That 1989 study conducted by the Center for Advanced Purchasing Studies (CAPS), *Purchasing from Small Minority-Owned Firms: Corporate Problems,* found that a combined sample composed of MBEs, CPPs, and Small Business Enterprises (SBEs), ranked undercapitalization as the *very least important* impediment item that MBEs face.

2. WBEs believe that they have more impediments to overcome than are perceived by the CPPs. Some of the impediments WBEs identified are: dealing in a sometimes unfriendly and tense environment; CPPs lack information about the WBEs' firms and their capabilities; WBEs face high costs in making CPPs aware of their availability; and that CPPs still rely on their "old-boy" networks in selecting suppliers. The CPPs identified a lack of information regarding the WBEs' businesses and their capabilities, and a lack of available WBEs as significant impediments to successfully conducting business with WBEs.

3. WBEs are confident in their ability to conduct business with their customers and

believe that they have the managerial and technical personnel to get their work accomplished in a timely and efficient manner, which includes producing quality products/services. CPPs, however, are slightly less confident of WBEs' ability.

4. WBEs believe that buyers have negative attitudes toward WBEs and make it difficult for WBEs to "get their foot in the door." CPPs, however, strongly disagree that this is an impediment to successfully conducting business.

5. The sales data collected from WBEs indicate that approximately 38 percent of the WBEs reported annual sales of $100,000 or less. These data suggest that many of these firms are just getting by and will find themselves under increasing strain to meet rising costs.

6. WBEs and CPPs generally agree upon the activities that can be employed to overcome the impediments to successful business. Some of the activities identified by both WBEs and CPPs are: train buyers in WBE problems; use a certification process; sponsor WBEs at business education programs; provide feedback to WBEs on bidding; publish lists of commodities and supply procedures; and assume a leading role in community economic development regarding women in business. These activities suggest that some common ground exists for helping WBEs to overcome the impediments they face.

7. Although WBEs and CPPs generally agree upon the activities, WBEs believe that all but one of the 28 activities will assist them in overcoming impediments, while CPPs perceive that 19 of the 28 activities will help WBEs overcome impediments. This finding would indicate that the WBEs believe that nearly every activity will be beneficial in overcoming impediments.

INTRODUCTION •

Women business ownership is increasing rapidly in the United States. Many recent articles and reports cite statistics that women own close to 30 percent of domestic businesses and are expected to own 36 percent by the year 2000, according to the U.S. Small Business Administration's Office of Advocacy. The importance of women business enterprises (WBEs) to the national economy is due to job creation and tax-revenue generation.[1]

To date, the laws at the federal and local levels have had, for the most part, an indiscernible effect on the growth and prosperity of WBEs. Government awareness was apparent when President Carter signed Executive Order 12138 on May 18, 1979, which created a National Women's Business Enterprise Policy and prescribed arrangements for developing, coordinating, and implementing a national program for women business enterprises.[2]

The Women's Business Ownership Act (PL 100-533), enacted on October 25, 1988, addressed several general areas: demonstration projects, access to capital, establishment of a national women's business council, and statistical data and effect on other programs.[3]

The laws mandating set-aside programs for minority-owned businesses have not been extended to WBEs. However, the legal landscape is changing. In 1989 Representative John LaFalce, D-N.Y., sponsored a bill that would require all federal agencies to develop annual goals for awarding contracts to small businesses owned by women. The bill (HR 3371), which was in hearings in mid-1990, also would require agencies to actively solicit bids from WBEs for all competitive contracts.[4]

In addition, President Bush pledged to increase business ownership opportunities for women. The U.S. Small Business Administration (SBA) has developed nine new initiatives to carry out the President's commitment to WBEs.

These nine initiatives fall into three major categories: (1) improve finance and procurement programs for women-owned firms (improve access to credit for WBEs, fully implement the "$50,000- or-less" small-loan program, increase prime contract awards to WBEs, and increase the number of subcontracting awards to WBEs from prime contractors); (2) increase training for female entrepreneurs (establish the women's network for entrepreneurial training [WNET] program in 50 states, increase representation of women on SBA's national and regional advisory councils, and increase recruitment and representation of women in key management and administrative positions at SBA); and (3) improve information and data about WBEs (increase information about demographics of WBEs, and support the work of the national women's business council).[5]

Senate Bill 1480, known as the Economic Equity Act of 1989, contains a section titled "Women's Business Procurement Assistance Act of 1989." Under the bill, corporations contracting with the federal government would be required to contract with and purchase from WBEs.[6] This arrangement closely parallels Public Law 95-507 of 1978, which requires contractors to submit subcontract plans to a proper federal agency and provide progress reports towards achieving specified percentages of business placed with small minority-owned firms.[7]

Many corporations not subject to federal legislation initiate WBE programs. Corporate motivation for WBE programs and other similar programs stems from a desire to develop a reliable supplier base, fulfill societal obligations, and stimulate employment for recognized socially and economically disadvantaged groups. However, the corporations often experience difficulties in their efforts to comply with legal requirements and to initiate programs of their own to help WBEs and similar groups. Often WBEs and CPPs find themselves disappointed with their failed attempts to transact business.

The purpose of this study is to reach a better understanding of the impediments large corporations face when buying from WBEs. Consequently, the perspectives of both the corporate purchasing personnel and the women business enterprises are examined.

This study is based on a theoretical framework known as the theory of transaction cost economics (TCE). TCE theory analyzes the interactions between transacting parties (WBEs and CPPs in this case) and attempts to identify the sources of transaction costs. Most important, TCE theory can be used to detect and measure an imbalance in transaction cost constraints that may exist between WBEs and CPPs.[8] This study examines these transaction costs, tests for any measurable imbalances, and offers solutions within the TCE framework to correct imbalances.

DESIGN OF THE STUDY   •

_____

STUDY GOALS

This study was sponsored by the Center for Advanced Purchasing Studies (CAPS). The primary objectives of this research were:

1. To determine the impediments to women business enterprise (WBE) purchasing programs.

2. To survey the extent to which WBEs and corporate purchasing personnel (CPPs) differed on these impediments.

3. To determine which activities to overcome the impediments were preferred by WBEs and which were preferred by corporate purchasing personnel (CPPs).

PHASES OF THE STUDY

The study was conducted in three distinct phases. The first phase assessed the current knowledge and practice in the area of women business enterprise by reviewing literature and previous studies and by conducting a series of interviews with women business owners.

The second phase involved the development of a survey instrument that was pretested on 35 randomly selected WBEs throughout the western United States. A revised survey instrument for both WBEs and CPPs was sent to representative samples nationwide.

The third phase involved data tabulation and analysis. The questions on the surveys were recombined into scales that represent the variables in the transaction cost economics (TCE) framework. The results and conclusions appear in the body of this report.

THE SAMPLE •

DATA

Fifteen women business enterprises (WBEs) were interviewed in the summer of 1988. A survey instrument was developed from the interviews and distributed to 400 WBEs chosen randomly from the 1988 edition of the *National Directory of Women-Owned Business Firms*.

Four hundred survey instruments were mailed, and 75 were returned by the WBEs, for a response rate of 18.6 percent. The WBE survey instruments that were returned represented 30 different two-digit SIC codes and 73 different three-digit ZIP codes.

Corporate purchasing personnel (CPPs) were sent a similar survey instrument. The firms these CPPs represented were selected from the Fortune 1000 list. Additional firms were also selected. All participants were chosen randomly. Five hundred fifty-five survey instruments were mailed, and 105 were returned, for an 18.9–percent response rate. The CPP survey instruments that were returned represented 25 different two-digit SIC codes and 91 different three-digit ZIP codes.

Respondents were asked to provide information about their race, education, job title, and number of years in current position. Table 2 summarizes the data.

TABLE 1
RESPONSE RATES AND PARTICIPATION

Group	Number of Surveys Mailed	Number of Surveys Returned	Response Rate
Women-Owned Firms (WBEs)	400	75	18.6%
Corporations (CPPs)	555	105	18.9%

Group	Number of Two-Digit SIC Codes	Number of Three-Digit ZIP Codes
Women-Owned Firms (WBEs)	30	73
Corporations (CPPs)	25	91

TABLE 2
CHARACTERISTICS OF THE RESPONDENTS

	WBE		CPP	
	#	%	#	%
Race:				
Black	2	2.6	3	2.9
Hispanic	4	5.3	1	1.0
Caucasian	54	72.0	91	86.7
Asian	3	4.0	3	2.9
Native American	7	9.3	4	3.8
Other/Not stated	5	6.7	3	2.9
Education:				
Less than high school	2	2.7	0	0
High school graduate	10	13.3	0	0
Some college	15	20.0	19	18.1
College graduate	21	28.0	35	33.3
Some graduate school	9	12.0	15	14.2
Graduate degree	17	22.7	34	32.3
Not stated	1	1.3	2	.9
Job Title (WBE):				
Owner	68	90.6		
Other	5	6.7		
Not stated	2	2.7		
Job Title (CPP):				
V.P. Purchasing			15	14.2
Director/Manager of Materials			10	9.5
Director/Manager of Purchasing			50	47.6
Buyer/Agent			5	4.7
Vendor Development Manager			13	12.4
Vendor Development Coordinator			6	5.7
Other			3	2.8
Not stated			3	2.8

	WBE	CPP
Number of Years in Current Position (Avg.):	9.7	7.3

CHARACTERISTICS OF THE RESPONDENTS

Table 2 profiles the characteristics of each of the two groups in the study. The major variables are: race, education, average years on the job, and title. These characteristics were collected from page 2 of both the WBE and CPP survey instruments. (See Appendix A.)

The WBE sample is primarily Caucasian (72.0%). There were 16 respondents in the WBE sample who identified themselves as representing a cultural or racial minority, such as Hispanic, Native American, Asian, or black. The other five respondents classified themselves as "other" or did not state their race.

As expected, the CPP sample is overwhelmingly Caucasian (86.7%). Another 11 respondents in the CPP sample identified themselves as Asian, Native American, black, or Hispanic. Three respondents classified themselves as "other" or did not state their race.

The second variable reported in Table 2 is education. More than half the respondents from each group had completed college, and 22.7 percent of the WBE respondents had earned graduate degrees, versus 32.3 percent of the CPP respondents.

There is little difference between the WBEs and the CPPs in the number of years on the job, 9.7 years versus 7.3 years respectively. The 9.7 years for the WBEs seems high. However, one explanation might be that the 75 responses were more likely to have come from successful WBEs; the unsuccessful WBEs were less likely to respond.

More than 71 percent of the CPP sample is composed of directors or vice-presidents. The percentage of WBE owners in the sample is 90.6 percent. Therefore, the people in the best position to know their firm's experience with corporate purchasing programs filled out the survey instrument.

WBEs and CPPs from all over the country and from many different types of businesses returned the survey instrument. (See Table 1.) Therefore, it can be concluded that the data collected in this study represent a valid cross section of opinion and experience.

SALES DATA

Sales data on WBE firms and corporations also were collected. Figures 1 and 2 present the results. Figure 1 indicates that about 38 percent of the WBEs (or 28 out of 74) reported annual sales of less than $100,000, and about 66 percent reported annual sales of less than $500,000. Sixteen percent of the WBE respondents had sales of $1 million or more.

Because the CPPs' firms have a larger sales volume, the scale in Figure 2 was changed, and Figure 1 cannot be directly compared with Figure 2. Figure 2 reveals that 33 out of 103 respondents (32%) had sales of $1,000,000,001 to $5 billion, while 40 of the CPP respondents (39%) reported sales of $1 billion or less.

FIGURE 1
WBE SALES DATA*

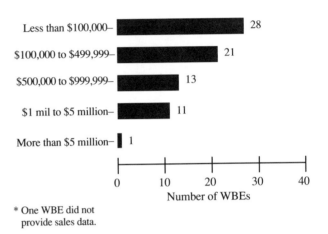

* One WBE did not provide sales data.

FIGURE 2
CPP SALES DATA*

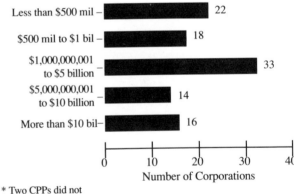

* Two CPPs did not provide sales data.

Additionally, WBEs were asked what percentage of their sales are due to being a WBE; the average response was 27.4 percent. Eleven of the 75 WBE respondents reported no figure for this question. CPPs were asked what percentage of their total purchasing dollars spent were allocated to WBEs; the average response was 2.1 percent. Thirty-three of the 105 CPP attempts to identify the sources of transaction costs. Most important, TCE theory can be used to detect and measure an imbalance in transaction cost constraints that may exist between WBEs and CPPs.[8] This study examines these transaction costs, tests for any measurable imbalances, and offers solutions within the TCE framework to correct imbalances.

DESIGN OF THE STUDY •

STUDY GOALS

This study was sponsored by the Center for Advanced Purchasing Studies (CAPS). The primary objectives of this research were:

1. To determine the impediments to women business enterprise (WBE) purchasing programs.

2. To survey the extent to which WBEs and corporate purchasing personnel (CPPs) differed on these impediments.

3. To determine which activities to overcome the impediments were preferred by WBEs and which were preferred by corporate purchasing personnel (CPPs).

PHASES OF THE STUDY

The study was conducted in three distinct phases. The first phase assessed the current knowledge and practice in the area of women business enterprise by reviewing literature and previous studies and by conducting a series of interviews with women business owners.

The second phase involved the development of a survey instrument that was pretested on 35 randomly selected WBEs throughout the western United States. A revised survey instrument for both WBEs and CPPs was sent to representative samples nationwide.

The third phase involved data tabulation and analysis. The questions on the surveys were recombined into scales that represent the variables in the transaction cost economics (TCE) framework. The results and conclusions appear in the body of this report.

THE SAMPLE •

DATA

Fifteen women business enterprises (WBEs) were interviewed in the summer of 1988. A survey instrument was developed from the interviews and distributed to 400 WBEs chosen randomly from the 1988 edition of the *National Directory of Women-Owned Business Firms.*

Four hundred survey instruments were mailed, and 75 were returned by the WBEs, for a response rate of 18.6 percent. The WBE survey instruments that were returned represented 30 different two-digit SIC codes and 73 different three-digit ZIP codes.

Corporate purchasing personnel (CPPs) were sent a similar survey instrument. The firms these CPPs represented were selected from the Fortune 1000 list. Additional firms were also selected. All participants were chosen randomly. Five hundred fifty-five survey instruments were mailed, and 105 were returned, for an 18.9–percent response rate. The CPP survey instruments that were returned represented 25 different two-digit SIC codes and 91 different three-digit ZIP codes.

TABLE 1
RESPONSE RATES AND PARTICIPATION

Group	Number of Surveys Mailed	Number of Surveys Returned	Response Rate
Women-Owned Firms (WBEs)	400	75	18.6%
Corporations (CPPs)	555	105	18.9%

Group	Number of Two-Digit SIC Codes	Number of Three-Digit ZIP Codes
Women-Owned Firms (WBEs)	30	73
Corporations (CPPs)	25	91

Respondents were asked to provide information about their race, education, job title, and number of years in current position. Table 2 summarizes the data.

TABLE 2
CHARACTERISTICS OF THE RESPONDENTS

	WBE #	WBE %	CPP #	CPP %
Race:				
Black	2	2.6	3	2.9
Hispanic	4	5.3	1	1.0
Caucasian	54	72.0	91	86.7
Asian	3	4.0	3	2.9
Native American	7	9.3	4	3.8
Other/Not stated	5	6.7	3	2.9
Education:				
Less than high school	2	2.7	0	0
High school graduate	10	13.3	0	0
Some college	15	20.0	19	18.1
College graduate	21	28.0	35	33.3
Some graduate school	9	12.0	15	14.2
Graduate degree	17	22.7	34	32.3
Not stated	1	1.3	2	.9
Job Title (WBE):				
Owner	68	90.6		
Other	5	6.7		
Not stated	2	2.7		
Job Title (CPP):				
V.P. Purchasing			15	14.2
Director/Manager of Materials			10	9.5
Director/Manager of Purchasing			50	47.6
Buyer/Agent			5	4.7
Vendor Development Manager			13	12.4
Vendor Development Coordinator			6	5.7
Other			3	2.8
Not stated			3	2.8

	WBE	CPP
Number of Years in Current Position (Avg.):	9.7	7.3

CHARACTERISTICS OF THE RESPONDENTS

Table 2 profiles the characteristics of each of the two groups in the study. The major variables are: race, education, average years on the job, and title. These characteristics were collected from page 2 of both the WBE and CPP survey instruments. (See Appendix A.)

The WBE sample is primarily Caucasian (72.0%). There were 16 respondents in the WBE sample who identified themselves as representing a cultural or racial minority, such as Hispanic, Native American, Asian, or black. The other five respondents classified themselves as "other" or did not state their race.

As expected, the CPP sample is overwhelmingly Caucasian (86.7%). Another 11 respondents in the CPP sample identified themselves as Asian, Native American, black, or Hispanic. Three respondents classified themselves as "other" or did not state their race.

The second variable reported in Table 2 is education. More than half the respondents from each group had completed college, and 22.7 percent of the WBE respondents had earned graduate degrees, versus 32.3 percent of the CPP respondents.

There is little difference between the WBEs and the CPPs in the number of years on the job, 9.7 years versus 7.3 years respectively. The 9.7 years for the WBEs seems high. However, one explanation might be that the 75 responses were more likely to have come from successful WBEs; the unsuccessful WBEs were less likely to respond.

More than 71 percent of the CPP sample is composed of directors or vice-presidents. The percentage of WBE owners in the sample is 90.6 percent. Therefore, the people in the best position to know their firm's experience with corporate purchasing programs filled out the survey instrument.

WBEs and CPPs from all over the country and from many different types of businesses returned the survey instrument. (See Table 1.) Therefore, it can be concluded that the data collected in this study represent a valid cross section of opinion and experience.

SALES DATA

Sales data on WBE firms and corporations also were collected. Figures 1 and 2 present the results. Figure 1 indicates that about 38 percent of the WBEs (or 28 out of 74) reported annual sales of less than $100,000, and about 66 percent reported annual sales of less than $500,000. Sixteen percent of the WBE respondents had sales of $1 million or more.

Because the CPPs' firms have a larger sales volume, the scale in Figure 2 was changed, and Figure 1 cannot be directly compared with Figure 2. Figure 2 reveals that 33 out of 103 respondents (32%) had sales of $1,000,000,001 to $5 billion, while 40 of the CPP respondents (39%) reported sales of $1 billion or less.

FIGURE 1
WBE SALES DATA*

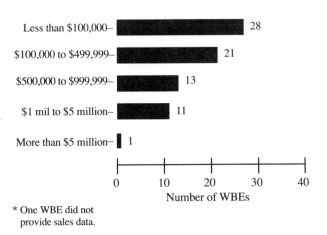

* One WBE did not provide sales data.

FIGURE 2
CPP SALES DATA*

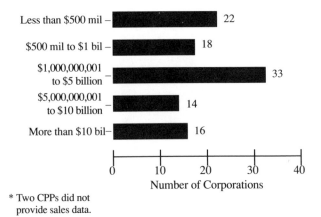

* Two CPPs did not provide sales data.

Additionally, WBEs were asked what percentage of their sales are due to being a WBE; the average response was 27.4 percent. Eleven of the 75 WBE respondents reported no figure for this question. CPPs were asked what percentage of their total purchasing dollars spent were allocated to WBEs; the average response was 2.1 percent. Thirty-three of the 105 CPP

I.10. Corporations don't give much feedback to WBEs.
I.13. Corporations take too long to pay.
I.15. WBEs are often undercapitalized.
I.17. WBEs are powerless to negotiate favorable terms.
I.19. Only small-volume orders are placed with WBEs.

Activity Variables

Monitoring of WBEs

A.6. Hold quality assurance meetings.
A.14. Train buyers in problems of WBEs.
A.15. Require performance bonds.
A.16. Perform credit checks/reference checks.

Monitoring of CPPs

A.12. Employ automated monitoring/tracking of WBE agreements.
A.17. Set specific purchasing target goals for WBEs.
A.18. Establish a WBE advocate program within the company.
A.19. High visibility and commendations for buyer participation.
A.20. Get top management involved.
A.21. Organize a permanent in-house task force.
A.23. Establish a WBE program in every department.

Searching for WBEs

A.8. Attend trade fairs for WBEs.
A.9. Place ads in women's entrepreneur publications.
A.11. Waive restrictive requirements.
A.13. Help with bid preparation and simplify the bidding process.
A.24. Employ automated data bases for WBE procurement and make a listing available to all departments.

Searching for CPPs

A.22. Take a leadership role in community economic development regarding women in business.
A.25. Disseminate long-term purchasing needs.
A.27. Publish a list of buyer names/ commodities and supply procedures.
A.28. List large-volume opportunities.

Financial Assistance

A.7. Offer loans or loan guarantees to WBEs.
A.10. Establish prepayment agreements.

Managerial Assistance

A.1. Provide or use a certification process.
A.2. Offer management assistance.
A.26. Provide feedback to unsuccessful bidders.

Technical Assistance

A.4. Give WBEs access to company technical resources.
A.13. Help with bid preparation and simplify the bidding process.

Cultural Interaction

A.14. Train buyers in problems of WBEs.

Internalization

A.3. Participate in joint ventures.
A.4. Give WBEs access to company technical resources.
A.5. Make company internal training available to WBEs.

Analysis of Impediments

The impediment variables have been ranked by their average scores based on the WBE/CPP survey instrument results. WBEs and CPPs were asked to rank the items on a seven-point scale. Scores of 4 indicate neither agreement nor disagreement with the item. As scores approach 1, respondents increasingly disagree that the item is an impediment. Conversely, as scores approach 7, the item is more apt to be viewed as an impediment. The rankings are shown in Figures 3 and 4.

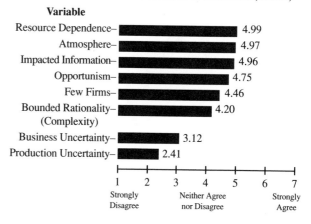

FIGURE 3
RANK ORDER OF IMPEDIMENT SCORES (WBEs)

FIGURE 4
RANK ORDER OF IMPEDIMENT SCORES (CPPs)

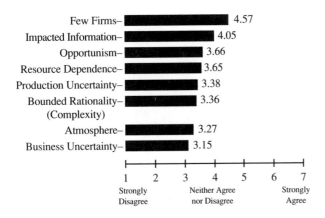

Variable

Few Firms– 4.57
Impacted Information– 4.05
Opportunism– 3.66
Resource Dependence– 3.65
Production Uncertainty– 3.38
Bounded Rationality– 3.36
(Complexity)
Atmosphere– 3.27
Business Uncertainty– 3.15

1 2 3 4 5 6 7

Strongly   Neither Agree   Strongly
Disagree   nor Disagree   Agree

Inferences can be drawn from the results found in Figures 3 and 4. The impediment variables consist of statements from the WBE/CPP survey. Tables 3 and 4 help to explain how the impediment items form the variables, how the items are ranked, and how the numerical scores are assigned to each.

Table 3 refers to the WBE sample and shows the rank order of the Top 10 impediment items, while Table 4 refers to the CPP sample and displays the data in a similar fashion. Both Tables 3 and 4 reflect the mean scores.

Figure 3 reveals that the primary impediment variable identified by WBEs was **Resource Dependence**. Table 3 suggests that at least three specific items contribute to this dependence: *WBEs are often undercapitalized, Only small-volume orders are placed with WBEs,* and *Corporations take too long to pay.*

Atmosphere is identified as an impediment variable with nearly the same score as that of **Resource Dependence.** The two items from Table 3

TABLE 3

IMPEDIMENT ITEMS —WBE SAMPLE

(TOP 10)

Rank	Item	Mean Score of Impediment Item	Variable*
1	WBEs are often undercapitalized.	5.81	Resource Dependence
2	Buyers rely on their "old-boy networks" in selecting suppliers.	5.72	Opportunism
3	It's difficult for WBEs to get their foot in the door.	5.54	Atmosphere
4	Buyers lack information on WBE capability.	5.46	Impacted Information
5	Buyers use WBEs just to satisfy statistics.	5.42	Opportunism
6	Only small-volume orders are placed with WBEs.	5.35	Resource Dependence
7	There is a lack of corporate commitment to WBE purchasing programs.	5.35	Opportunism
8	Buyers don't know much about WBEs' business.	5.33	Impacted Information/ Bounded Rationality (Complexity)
9	Corporations take too long to pay.	5.21	Resource Dependence
10	Buyers don't work closely with WBEs.	5.21	Atmosphere

*Variables were created out of the items in the survey instrument to represent the dimensions of the transaction-cost framework.

that contribute heavily to the impediment variable **Atmosphere** are: *It's difficult for WBEs to get their foot in the door*, and *Buyers don't work closely with WBEs*.

Impacted Information ranks third in the list of impediment variables in Figure 3. As Table 3 indicates, WBEs believe that *Buyers lack information on WBE capability*, and *Buyers don't know much about WBEs' business*.

Figure 3 indicates that WBEs perceive that six of the eight variables are impediments, while Figure 4 reveals that CPPs perceive only two of the eight variables are impediments.

Figure 4 reveals that **Few Firms** was the primary impediment variable according to CPPs. The data in Table 4 suggest that only two of the three items that make up the **Few Firms** variable were perceived by the CPPs as being impediments to doing business with WBEs: *Buyers are not aware of available WBEs, and WBEs are not available in specialized areas.*

CPPs also identified **Impacted Information** as an impediment variable. Specifically, the impediment items contributing to **Impacted Information's** high ranking are: *Buyers lack information on WBE capability, Buyers don't know much about WBEs' business*, and *Corporations don't get the word out about their programs*. WBEs and CPPs both agree that buyers lack information about WBE capabilities and knowledge about WBEs' businesses.

Comparisons between Figures 3 and 4 reveal that the WBEs' ranking of variables shows a wider range than does the CPPs' ranking. The mean scores in the WBE sample range from a high of 4.99 to a low of 2.41, while mean scores in the CPP sample range from a high of 4.57 to a low of 3.15. An explanation follows for the wide range in the WBE and CPP rankings.

TABLE 4

IMPEDIMENT ITEMS—CPP SAMPLE

(TOP 10)

Rank	Item	Mean Score of Impediment Item	Variable*
1	Buyers are not aware of available WBEs.	4.86	Few Firms
2	WBEs are not available in specialized areas.	4.85	Few Firms
3	Buyers lack information on WBE capability.	4.71	Impacted Information
4	WBEs are often undercapitalized.	4.61	Resource Dependence
5	Buyers don't know much about WBEs' business.	4.38	Impacted Information/ Bounded Rationality (Complexity)
6	Corporations don't get the word out about their programs.	4.32	Impacted Information
7	WBEs could be acting as a "front" for non-women business.	4.32	Opportunism
8	WBEs need technical assistance.	4.15	Resource Dependence
9	There is a lack of corporate commitment to WBE purchasing programs.	4.13	Opportunism
10	The government doesn't enforce the regulations on WBE purchasing.	4.10	Bounded Rationality (Complexity)

*Variables were created out of the items in the survey instrument to represent the dimensions of the transaction-cost framework.

Six of the variables in Figure 3 have a mean score of more than 4.00 and are perceived by the WBEs as being impediments to successful business transactions, **Resource Dependence** (4.99), **Atmosphere** (4.97), **Impacted Information** (4.96), **Opportunism** (4.75), **Few Firms** (4.46), and **Bounded Rationality (Complexity)** (4.20). WBEs assigned lower scores to **Business Uncertainty** (3.12) and **Production Uncertainty** (2.41), which indicates that WBEs have confidence in the way they conduct business with their customers and doubt that these variables are impediments.

The CPPs, however, rank two of the eight variables, **Few Firms** (4.57) and **Impacted Information** (4.05) as having mean scores of more than 4.00. The CPPs perceive that the remaining six variables in Figure 4, **Opportunism** (3.66), **Resource Dependence** (3.65), **Production Uncertainty** (3.38), **Bounded Rationality (Complexity)** (3.36), **Atmosphere** (3.27), and **Business Uncertainty** (3.15), are *not* impediments and assign them mean scores of less than 4.00.

These data suggest that the WBEs and the CPPs disagree sharply on which variables are impediments, thus accounting for the wide range in mean scores found in Figures 3 and 4.

Further comparison of Figures 3 and 4 shows that WBEs and CPPs differ strongly concerning the variables **Resource Dependence** and **Atmosphere**. WBEs rank **Resource Dependence** as the most important impediment variable with a mean score of 4.99, while CPPs rank it fourth with an average of only 3.65. A comparison of Tables 3 and 4 shows that *WBEs are often undercapitalized* (one of the impediment items that constitute the variable **Resource Dependence**) accounts for much of the difference in variable ranking because WBEs and CPPs differ so widely on this particular item (5.81 versus 4.61).

The **Atmosphere** variable shows an even greater difference, as the average for WBEs was 4.97 versus a score of 3.27 for CPPs. Table 3 indicates that items 3, *It's difficult for WBEs to get their foot in the door*, and 10, *Buyers don't work closely with WBEs*, contribute strongly to the overall 4.97 score. Comparatively, the data in Table 4 show that the **Atmosphere** variable does not even appear in the Top 10 of the CPP sample.

A report similar to the WBE report titled *Purchasing from Small Minority-Owned Firms: Corporate Problems* was published in 1989 by

CAPS. It reveals that a combined sample of minority-owned business enterprises (MBEs), small business enterprises (SBEs), and corporate purchasing personnel (CPPs) ranked the impediment item *MBEs are often undercapitalized* as the lowest impediment, with a mean score of 2.58. By contrast, the WBEs and the CPPs in the WBE report ranked the impediment item *WBEs are often undercapitalized* first and fourth in importance. (See Tables 3 and 4.) The mean score of 5.81 assigned by the WBEs to this impediment item indicates that WBEs believe that having too little capital for efficient operation of their businesses is the largest single impediment to conducting business successfully. The CPPs agree that undercapitalization of women business enterprises is an impediment, and they gave it a lower ranking of 4.61. (See Table 4.)

Tables 5 and 6 display the Bottom 10 impediment items for WBEs and CPPs respectively. Table 5 indicates that WBEs do not believe the variables **Production Uncertainty** and **Business Uncertainty** are impediments. Seven of the 10 impediment items that WBEs ranked relate to either **Production Uncertainty** or **Business Uncertainty**.

These scores indicate that the WBEs appear confident in their ability to produce quality output efficiently and effectively, and in their ability to perform and survive over time. CPPs agree somewhat with WBEs regarding these variables as reported in Table 6. Four of the Bottom 10 impediment items relate to either **Production Uncertainty** or **Business Uncertainty**.

A comparison of Tables 5 and 6 shows that CPPs assigned slightly higher scores to their lowest-10-ranked impediment items. Also, both WBEs and CPPs appear to rank **Bounded Rationality (Complexity)** as a variable that does not represent a significant impediment.

Analysis of Activity Variables

Respondents provided rankings for a set of activity variables. The activity variables are actions intended to overcome the impediment variables. These activities and their relationships to the impediments were discussed previously in this report.

The activity variables have been ranked by their average scores based on the WBE/CPP survey instrument results. The rankings are shown in Figures 5 and 6.

TABLE 5

IMPEDIMENT ITEMS—WBE SAMPLE

(BOTTOM 10)

Rank	Item	Mean Score of Impediment Item	Variable*
32	WBEs have a "give-me" attitude.	3.14	Opportunism
33	WBE programs lead buyers to compromise their professional standards.	3.03	Bounded Rationality (Complexity)
34	WBEs have poor bidding practices.	2.91	Bounded Rationality (Complexity)
35	Performance by WBEs is too uncertain.	2.66	Business Uncertainty
36	WBEs lack qualified technical personnel.	2.58	Production Uncertainty
37	WBEs lack qualified managerial personnel.	2.57	Business Uncertainty
38	WBEs lack qualified sales personnel.	2.51	Business Uncertainty
39	WBEs can't meet bid/quote deadlines.	2.48	Business Uncertainty
40	WBEs have inefficient production capacities.	2.41	Production Uncertainty
41	WBEs need long lead times to correct quality problems.	2.26	Production Uncertainty

*Variables were created out of the items in the survey instrument to represent the dimensions of the transaction-cost framework.

TABLE 6

IMPEDIMENT ITEMS —CPP SAMPLE

(BOTTOM 10)

Rank	Item	Mean Score of Impediment Item	Variable*
32	WBEs have difficulty advertising their products/services.	3.09	Impacted Information
33	Performance by WBEs is too uncertain.	3.06	Business Uncertainty
34	WBEs need long lead times to correct quality problems.	3.05	Production Uncertainty
35	WBEs have poor bidding practices.	3.01	Bounded Rationality (Complexity)
36	WBEs can't meet bid/quote deadlines.	2.64	Business Uncertainty
37	Sexism is prevalent in corporations doing business with WBEs.	2.60	Atmosphere
38	Buyer turnover is too high to establish long-term relationships with WBEs.	2.60	Bounded Rationality (Complexity)
39	Doing business with large corporations is not very profitable for WBEs.	2.50	Business Uncertainty
40	WBEs are powerless to negotiate favorable terms.	2.36	Resource Dependence
41	WBE programs lead buyers to compromise their professional standards.	2.16	Bounded Rationality (Complexity)

*Variables were created out of the items in the survey instrument to represent the dimensions of the transaction-cost framework.

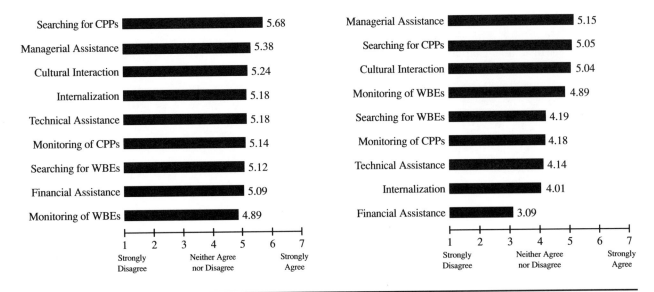

FIGURE 5

RANK ORDER OF ACTIVITY SCORES (WBEs)

Searching for CPPs	5.68
Managerial Assistance	5.38
Cultural Interaction	5.24
Internalization	5.18
Technical Assistance	5.18
Monitoring of CPPs	5.14
Searching for WBEs	5.12
Financial Assistance	5.09
Monitoring of WBEs	4.89

1 Strongly Disagree 2 3 4 Neither Agree nor Disagree 5 6 7 Strongly Agree

FIGURE 6

RANK ORDER OF ACTIVITY SCORES (CPPs)

Managerial Assistance	5.15
Searching for CPPs	5.05
Cultural Interaction	5.04
Monitoring of WBEs	4.89
Searching for WBEs	4.19
Monitoring of CPPs	4.18
Technical Assistance	4.14
Internalization	4.01
Financial Assistance	3.09

1 Strongly Disagree 2 3 4 Neither Agree nor Disagree 5 6 7 Strongly Agree

TABLE 7

ACTIVITY ITEMS—WBE SAMPLE

(TOP 10)

Rank	Item	Mean Score of Activity Item	Variable*
1	List large-volume opportunities.	5.89	Searching for CPPs
2	Provide feedback to unsuccessful bidders.	5.87	Managerial Assistance
3	Get top management involved.	5.85	Monitoring of CPPs
4	Publish a list of buyer names/commodities and supply procedures.	5.67	Searching for CPPs
5	High visibility and commendations for buyer participation.	5.63	Monitoring of CPPs
6	Take a leadership role in community economic development regarding women in business.	5.61	Searching for CPPs
7	Disseminate long-term purchasing needs.	5.55	Searching for CPPs
8	Employ automated data bases for WBE procurement and make a listing available to all departments.	5.47	Searching for WBEs
9	Participate in joint ventures.	5.37	Internalization
10	Establish a WBE advocate program within the company.	5.34	Monitoring of CPPs

*Variables were created out of the items in the survey instrument to represent the dimensions of the transaction-cost framework.

Inferences can be drawn from the results found in Figures 5 and 6. Tables 7 and 8 help to explain how the activity items form the variables, how the items are ranked, and the numerical scores assigned to each activity item.

Table 7 refers to the WBE sample and shows the rank order of the Top 10 activity items, while Table 8 refers to the CPP sample and displays the data in a similar fashion. Both Tables 7 and 8 show the mean scores for the Top 10 activity items.

Figure 5 shows that **Searching for CPPs** is the activity item that is ranked first by WBEs.

Managerial Assistance ranks second, followed by **Cultural Interaction**. Table 7 provides some explanation for these rankings. The activity item that contributes most to the high ranking of **Searching for CPPs** is *List large-volume opportunities*; the WBE respondents rank it number one, with a mean score of 5.89. Two other activity items among the Top 10 include *Take a leadership role in community economic development regarding women in business* (5.61) and *Disseminate long-term purchasing needs* (5.55).

Managerial Assistance ranks second among the activity variables, with a mean score of 5.38. The

TABLE 8

ACTIVITY ITEMS—CPP SAMPLE

(TOP 10)

Rank	Item	Mean Score of Activity Item	Variable*
1	Provide feedback to unsuccessful bidders.	5.82	Managerial Assistance
2	Publish a list of buyer names/commodities and supply procedures.	5.78	Searching for CPPs
3	Attend trade fairs for WBEs.	5.64	Searching for WBEs
4	Hold quality assurance meetings.	5.62	Monitoring of WBEs
5	Perform credit checks/reference checks.	5.30	Monitoring of WBEs
6	Provide or use a certification process.	5.28	Managerial Assistance
7	List large-volume opportunities.	5.06	Searching for CPPs
8	Train buyers in problems of WBEs.	5.04	Monitoring of WBEs/ Cultural Interaction
9	Get top management involved.	4.97	Monitoring of CPPs
10	Disseminate long-term purchasing needs.	4.97	Searching for CPPs

*Variables were created out of the items in the survey instrument to represent the dimensions of the transaction-cost framework.

activity item *Provide feedback to unsuccessful bidders* (5.87) was one of the key activity item statements (Table 7) that produced the mean score of 5.38. (See **Managerial Assistance,** Figure 5.)

Figure 5 also shows that WBEs rank **Cultural Interaction** third. This variable contains only one activity item, *Train buyers in problems of WBEs,* which is ranked number 13 with a mean score of 5.24. (See Appendix B.)

Figure 6 lists the rank order of mean score activity variables for CPPs. **Managerial Assistance** ranks first, with a score of 5.15. The specific activity item contributing most heavily to this ranking is *Provide feedback to unsuccessful bidders,* with a ranking of 5.82 in Table 8. Another activity item among the Top 10 is *Provide or use a certification process,* with a mean score of 5.28.

Figure 6 shows that the second-highest-ranking activity variable is **Searching for CPPs,** with a mean score of 5.05. The CPPs ranked three activity items as providing the most assistance to WBEs in their search for CPPs: *Publish a list of buyer names/commodities and supply procedures* (5.78), *List large-volume opportunities* (5.06), and *Disseminate long-term purchasing needs* (4.97).

While CPPs assigned the mean score of 5.04 to **Cultural Interaction,** WBEs gave it a slightly higher score of 5.24. Both WBEs and CPPs ranked **Cultural Interaction** third among activities to overcome impediments.

A comparative analysis of Figures 5 and 6 indicates that WBEs and CPPs rank **Managerial Assistance, Searching for CPPs,** and **Cultural Interaction** as the top three activity variables, although in a slightly different order. The mean scores assigned by the WBEs and the CPPs to the activity items show that both parties are somewhat in agreement with the activities that will assist them in overcoming the impediments. Five of the Top 10 activity items are common to both tables: *List large-volume opportunities, Provide feedback to unsuccessful bidders, Get top management involved, Publish a list of buyer names/commodities and supply procedures,* and *Disseminate long-term purchasing needs.*

Further comparisons between Figures 5 and 6 reveal that mean scores for WBEs are higher than are those for CPPs, and that a wider range exists in the CPP scores. The greater range of mean scores in the CPP sample perhaps is due to the very low average reported for **Financial Assistance** (3.09). CPPs believe that loans, loan guarantees, or prepayment

agreements will not assist WBEs in overcoming the impediments they face in this area of **Financial Assistance**.

It is interesting to note that, in Table 4, CPPs rank *WBEs are often undercapitalized* as the fourth impediment item (score of 4.61). However, in Figure 6, CPPs rank the activity variable **Financial Assistance** ninth (mean score of 3.09). This may indicate that neither the CPPs nor their organizations are capable of helping the WBEs overcome this impediment.

Considerable variance exists between the reported averages in Figures 5 and 6 for **Internalization** and **Financial Assistance**. The WBEs' average score for **Internalization** is 5.09 versus 4.01 for CPPs. One of the main reasons for this difference is that the two parties disagree sharply about the value of *Participate in joint ventures.* (See Tables 7 and 10.) WBEs assigned a mean score of 5.37 to this activity item; CPPs assigned it a value of only 3.97.

Tables 9 and 10 display the activity items ranked in the Bottom 10. Both WBEs and CPPs believe these activities to be least helpful in overcoming impediments. Of the activity items in Tables 9 and 10, nine activity items are common to both tables but are ordered differently on each table.

WBEs ranked the nine activity items common to both tables with higher mean scores than did the CPPs. The higher mean scores indicate that the WBEs believed that even the least helpful activities were still somewhat beneficial in overcoming impediments. Only one activity item listed in Table 9, *Require performance bonds* (3.85) had a mean score lower than 4.00, which indicates that the WBEs believed that all other activities were helpful in overcoming impediments.

Table 10 shows that the CPPs gave their Bottom 10 activity items lower mean scores overall than did the WBEs. Because only one activity item in the Bottom 10 received a score of more than 4.00, *Employ automated monitoring/tracking of WBE agreements* (4.16), CPPs apparently question whether any of the remaining Bottom 10 activity items would assist WBEs in overcoming impediments.

CPPs ranked *Waive restrictive requirements* (2.65) as the least helpful activity to overcome the impediments faced by WBEs. (See Table 10.) WBEs disagreed and assigned the mean score of 4.50 to this activity item, which indicates that WBEs perceive that this activity would assist them in overcoming the impediments. (See Table 9.)

WOMEN BUSINESS ENTERPRISE PURCHASING PROGRAM SURVEY

Instructions: Below is a list of statements that may be used to describe problems facing Women Business Enterprise (WBE) purchasing programs. Read each statement carefully and think about your own company. Then indicate whether you (1) Strongly Disagree, (2) Moderately Disagree, (3) Slightly Disagree, (4) Neither Agree nor Disagree, (5) Slightly Agree, (6) Moderately Agree, or (7) Strongly Agree with the statement by circling the appropriate number.

1 Strongly Disagree	2 Moderately Disagree	3 Slightly Disagree	4 Neither Agree Nor Disagree	5 Slightly Agree	6 Moderately Agree	7 Strongly Agree

1. Doing business with large corporations is not very profitable for WBEs. 1 2 3 4 5 6 7
2. WBEs have difficulty advertising their products/services. 1 2 3 4 5 6 7
3. Corporations don't get the word out about their programs. 1 2 3 4 5 6 7
4. The designation of "women business" hurts WBEs. 1 2 3 4 5 6 7
5. WBEs can't compete with bigger firms. 1 2 3 4 5 6 7
6. Buyers don't know much about WBEs' business. 1 2 3 4 5 6 7
7. WBEs need technical assistance. 1 2 3 4 5 6 7
8. Buyers use WBEs just to satisfy statistics. 1 2 3 4 5 6 7
9. Buyers don't work closely with WBEs. 1 2 3 4 5 6 7
10. Corporations don't give much feedback to WBEs. 1 2 3 4 5 6 7
11. Sexism is prevalent in corporations doing business with WBEs. 1 2 3 4 5 6 7
12. Obtaining required insurance is a problem for WBEs. 1 2 3 4 5 6 7
13. Corporations take too long to pay. 1 2 3 4 5 6 7
14. It's difficult for WBEs to get their foot in the door. 1 2 3 4 5 6 7
15. WBEs are often undercapitalized. 1 2 3 4 5 6 7
16. There is a lack of corporate commitment to WBE purchasing programs. 1 2 3 4 5 6 7
17. WBEs are powerless to negotiate favorable terms. 1 2 3 4 5 6 7
18. Buyers rely on their "old-boy networks" in selecting suppliers. 1 2 3 4 5 6 7
19. Only small-volume orders are placed with WBEs. 1 2 3 4 5 6 7
20. The government doesn't enforce the regulations on WBE purchasing. 1 2 3 4 5 6 7
21. WBEs are not available in specialized areas. 1 2 3 4 5 6 7
22. Buyers are not aware of available WBEs. 1 2 3 4 5 6 7
23. WBEs are not price-competitive. 1 2 3 4 5 6 7
24. Buyers lack information on WBE capability. 1 2 3 4 5 6 7
25. WBEs can't meet bid/quote deadlines. 1 2 3 4 5 6 7
26. Buyers have no incentive to make WBE purchasing programs work. 1 2 3 4 5 6 7
27. WBEs have a "give-me" attitude. 1 2 3 4 5 6 7
28. The WBE purchasing program is all politics. 1 2 3 4 5 6 7
29. Performance by WBEs is too uncertain. 1 2 3 4 5 6 7
30. WBEs have poor bidding practices. 1 2 3 4 5 6 7
31. Buyers have negative attitudes toward WBEs. 1 2 3 4 5 6 7
32. Resources to develop WBEs into reliable suppliers are not available. 1 2 3 4 5 6 7
33. Identifying and qualifying WBEs is a costly process. 1 2 3 4 5 6 7
34. Buyer turnover is too high to establish long-term relationships with WBEs. 1 2 3 4 5 6 7
35. WBE programs lead buyers to compromise their professional standards. 1 2 3 4 5 6 7
36. WBEs could be acting as a "front" for non-women business. 1 2 3 4 5 6 7
37. WBEs lack qualified technical personnel. 1 2 3 4 5 6 7
38. WBEs lack qualified managerial personnel. 1 2 3 4 5 6 7
39. WBEs lack qualified sales personnel. 1 2 3 4 5 6 7
40. WBEs have inefficient production capacities. 1 2 3 4 5 6 7
41. WBEs need long lead times to correct quality problems. 1 2 3 4 5 6 7

Instructions: Below is a list of activities that large companies might use to implement aspects of Women Business Enterprise (WBE) purchasing programs. Read each statement carefully and think about your own company. Then indicate whether you (1) **Strongly Disagree**, (2) **Moderately Disagree**, (3) **Slightly Disagree**, (4) **Neither Agree nor Disagree**, (5) **Slightly Agree**, (6) **Moderately Agree**, or (7) **Strongly Agree** that the activity should be part of a large company's WBE program.

1 Strongly Disagree	2 Moderately Disagree	3 Slightly Disagree	4 Neither Agree Nor Disagree	5 Slightly Agree	6 Moderately Agree	7 Strongly Agree

1. Provide or use a certification process.   1 2 3 4 5 6 7
2. Offer management assistance.   1 2 3 4 5 6 7
3. Participate in joint ventures.   1 2 3 4 5 6 7
4. Give WBEs access to company technical resources.   1 2 3 4 5 6 7
5. Make company internal training available to WBEs.   1 2 3 4 5 6 7
6. Hold quality assurance meetings.   1 2 3 4 5 6 7
7. Offer loans or loan guarantees to WBEs.   1 2 3 4 5 6 7
8. Attend trade fairs for WBEs.   1 2 3 4 5 6 7
9. Place ads in women's entrepreneur publications.   1 2 3 4 5 6 7
10. Establish prepayment agreements.   1 2 3 4 5 6 7
11. Waive restrictive requirements.   1 2 3 4 5 6 7
12. Employ automated monitoring/tracking of WBE agreements.   1 2 3 4 5 6 7
13. Help with bid preparation and simplify the bidding process.   1 2 3 4 5 6 7
14. Train buyers in problems of WBEs.   1 2 3 4 5 6 7
15. Require performance bonds.   1 2 3 4 5 6 7
16. Perform credit checks/reference checks.   1 2 3 4 5 6 7
17. Set specific purchasing target goals for WBEs.   1 2 3 4 5 6 7
18. Establish a WBE advocate program within the company.   1 2 3 4 5 6 7
19. High visibility and commendations for buyer participation.   1 2 3 4 5 6 7
20. Get top management involved.   1 2 3 4 5 6 7
21. Organize a permanent in-house task force.   1 2 3 4 5 6 7
22. Take a leadership role in community economic development regarding women in business.   1 2 3 4 5 6 7
23. Establish a WBE program in every department.   1 2 3 4 5 6 7
24. Employ automated data bases for WBE procurement and make a listing available to all departments.   1 2 3 4 5 6 7
25. Disseminate long-term purchasing needs.   1 2 3 4 5 6 7
26. Provide feedback to unsuccessful bidders.   1 2 3 4 5 6 7
27. Publish a list of buyer names/commodities and supply procedures.   1 2 3 4 5 6 7
28. List large-volume opportunities.   1 2 3 4 5 6 7

Job Title: _____ Owner; Other (please specify) _____

Years in Current Position: _____

Race/Origin: _____Black _____Hispanic _____Caucasian _____Asian _____Nat. American

Level of Education: _____less than high school _____high school graduate

      _____some college _____college degree

      _____some graduate work _____graduate degree

What percentage of your sales is due to being a Women Business Enterprise? _____%

Approximate total annual sales, 1988: (check one)

_____less than $100,000 _____$100,000 to $499,999 _____$500,000 to $999,999

_____$1 million to $5 million _____more than $5 million

WOMEN BUSINESS ENTERPRISE PURCHASING PROGRAM SURVEY

Instructions: Below is a list of statements that may be used to describe problems facing Women Business Enterprise (WBE) purchasing programs. Read each statement carefully and think about your own company. Then indicate whether you (1) Strongly Disagree, (2) Moderately Disagree, (3) Slightly Disagree, (4) Neither Agree nor Disagree, (5) Slightly Agree, (6) Moderately Agree, or (7) Strongly Agree with the statement by circling the appropriate number.

1	2	3	4	5	6	7
Strongly Disagree	Moderately Disagree	Slightly Disagree	Neither Agree Nor Disagree	Slightly Agree	Moderately Agree	Strongly Agree

1. Doing business with large corporations is not very profitable for WBEs. 1 2 3 4 5 6 7
2. WBEs have difficulty advertising their products/services. 1 2 3 4 5 6 7
3. Corporations don't get the word out about their programs. 1 2 3 4 5 6 7
4. The designation of "women business" hurts WBEs. 1 2 3 4 5 6 7
5. WBEs can't compete with bigger firms. 1 2 3 4 5 6 7
6. Buyers don't know much about WBEs' business. 1 2 3 4 5 6 7
7. WBEs need technical assistance. 1 2 3 4 5 6 7
8. Buyers use WBEs just to satisfy statistics. 1 2 3 4 5 6 7
9. Buyers don't work closely with WBEs. 1 2 3 4 5 6 7
10. Corporations don't give much feedback to WBEs. 1 2 3 4 5 6 7
11. Sexism is prevalent in corporations doing business with WBEs. 1 2 3 4 5 6 7
12. Obtaining required insurance is a problem for WBEs. 1 2 3 4 5 6 7
13. Corporations take too long to pay. 1 2 3 4 5 6 7
14. It's difficult for WBEs to get their foot in the door. 1 2 3 4 5 6 7
15. WBEs are often undercapitalized. 1 2 3 4 5 6 7
16. There is a lack of corporate commitment to WBE purchasing programs. 1 2 3 4 5 6 7
17. WBEs are powerless to negotiate favorable terms. 1 2 3 4 5 6 7
18. Buyers rely on their "old boy networks" in selecting suppliers. 1 2 3 4 5 6 7
19. Only small-volume orders are placed with WBEs. 1 2 3 4 5 6 7
20. The government doesn't enforce the regulations on WBE purchasing. 1 2 3 4 5 6 7
21. WBEs are not available in specialized areas. 1 2 3 4 5 6 7
22. Buyers are not aware of available WBEs. 1 2 3 4 5 6 7
23. WBEs are not price-competitive. 1 2 3 4 5 6 7
24. Buyers lack information on WBE capability. 1 2 3 4 5 6 7
25. WBEs can't meet bid/quote deadlines. 1 2 3 4 5 6 7
26. Buyers have no incentive to make WBE purchasing programs work. 1 2 3 4 5 6 7
27. WBEs have a "give-me" attitude. 1 2 3 4 5 6 7
28. The WBE purchasing program is all politics. 1 2 3 4 5 6 7
29. Performance by WBEs is too uncertain. 1 2 3 4 5 6 7
30. WBEs have poor bidding practices. 1 2 3 4 5 6 7
31. Buyers have negative attitudes toward WBEs. 1 2 3 4 5 6 7
32. Resources to develop WBEs into reliable suppliers are not available. 1 2 3 4 5 6 7
33. Identifying and qualifying WBEs is a costly process. 1 2 3 4 5 6 7
34. Buyer turnover is too high to establish long-term relationships with WBEs. 1 2 3 4 5 6 7
35. WBE programs lead buyers to compromise their professional standards. 1 2 3 4 5 6 7
36. WBEs could be acting as a "front" for non-women business. 1 2 3 4 5 6 7
37. WBEs lack qualified technical personnel. 1 2 3 4 5 6 7
38. WBEs lack qualified managerial personnel. 1 2 3 4 5 6 7
39. WBEs lack qualified sales personnel. 1 2 3 4 5 6 7
40. WBEs have inefficient production capacities. 1 2 3 4 5 6 7
41. WBEs need long lead times to correct quality problems. 1 2 3 4 5 6 7

Instructions: Below is a list of activities that large companies might use to implement aspects of Women Business Enterprise (WBE) purchasing programs. Read each statement carefully and think about your own company. Then indicate whether you (1) **Strongly Disagree**, (2) **Moderately Disagree**, (3) **Slightly Disagree**, (4) **Neither Agree nor Disagree**, (5) **Slightly Agree**, (6) **Moderately Agree**, or (7) **Strongly Agree** that the activity should be part of a large company's WBE program.

1	2	3	4	5	6	7
Strongly Disagree	Moderately Disagree	Slightly Disagree	Neither Agree Nor Disagree	Slightly Agree	Moderately Agree	Strongly Agree

1. Provide or use a certification process.   1 2 3 4 5 6 7
2. Offer management assistance.   1 2 3 4 5 6 7
3. Participate in joint ventures.   1 2 3 4 5 6 7
4. Give WBEs access to company technical resources.   1 2 3 4 5 6 7
5. Make company internal training available to WBEs.   1 2 3 4 5 6 7
6. Hold quality assurance meetings.   1 2 3 4 5 6 7
7. Offer loans or loan guarantees to WBEs.   1 2 3 4 5 6 7
8. Attend trade fairs for WBEs.   1 2 3 4 5 6 7
9. Place ads in women's entrepreneur publications.   1 2 3 4 5 6 7
10. Establish prepayment agreements.   1 2 3 4 5 6 7
11. Waive restrictive requirements.   1 2 3 4 5 6 7
12. Employ automated monitoring/tracking of WBE agreements.   1 2 3 4 5 6 7
13. Help with bid preparation and simplify the bidding process.   1 2 3 4 5 6 7
14. Train buyers in problems of WBEs.   1 2 3 4 5 6 7
15. Require performance bonds.   1 2 3 4 5 6 7
16. Perform credit checks/reference checks.   1 2 3 4 5 6 7
17. Set specific purchasing target goals for WBEs.   1 2 3 4 5 6 7
18. Establish a WBE advocate program within the company.   1 2 3 4 5 6 7
19. High visibility and commendations for buyer participation.   1 2 3 4 5 6 7
20. Get top management involved.   1 2 3 4 5 6 7
21. Organize a permanent in-house task force.
22. Take a leadership role in community economic development regarding women in business.   1 2 3 4 5 6 7
23. Establish a WBE program in every department.   1 2 3 4 5 6 7
24. Employ automated data bases for WBE procurement and make a listing available to all departments.   1 2 3 4 5 6 7
25. Disseminate long-term purchasing needs.   1 2 3 4 5 6 7
26. Provide feedback to unsuccessful bidders.   1 2 3 4 5 6 7
27. Publish a list of buyer names/commodities and supply procedures.   1 2 3 4 5 6 7
28. List large volume opportunities.   1 2 3 4 5 6 7

Your Job Title_____

Years in Current Position_____

Race/Origin: _____Black _____Hispanic _____Caucasian _____Asian _____Nat. American

Level of Education: _____less than high school _____high school graduate

      _____some college _____college degree

      _____some graduate work _____graduate degree

What percentage of your total purchasing dollars spent is allocated to Women Business Enterprises? _____%

Approximate total annual sales, 1988: (check one)

_____less than $500 million _____$500 million to $1 billion

_____$1,000,000,001 to $5 billion _____$5,000,000,001 to $10 billion

_____more than $10 billion

32

WOMEN BUSINESS ENTERPRISE PURCHASING PROGRAM SURVEY

__Instructions:__ Below is a list of statements that may be used to describe
problems facing Women Business Enterprise (WBE) purchasing programs. Read each statement
carefully and think about your own company. Then indicate whether you (1) Strongly
Disagree, (2) Moderately Disagree, (3) Slightly Disagree, (4) Neither Agree nor Disagree,
(5) Slightly Agree, (6) Moderately Agree, or (7) Strongly Agree with the statement by
circling the appropriate number.

1 Strongly Disagree	2 Moderately Disagree	3 Slightly Disagree	4 Neither Agree Nor Disagree	5 Slightly Agree	6 Moderately Agree	7 Strongly Agree

1. Doing business with large corporations is not very
   profitable for WBEs.
2. WBEs have difficulty advertising their products/services.   1 2 3 4 5 6 7
3. Corporations don't get the word out about their programs.   1 2 3 4 5 6 7
4. The designation of "women business" hurts WBEs.   1 2 3 4 5 6 7
5. WBEs can't compete with bigger firms.   1 2 3 4 5 6 7
6. Buyers don't know much about WBEs' business.   1 2 3 4 5 6 7
7. WBEs need technical assistance.   1 2 3 4 5 6 7
8. Buyers use WBEs just to satisfy statistics.   1 2 3 4 5 6 7
9. Buyers don't work closely with WBEs.   1 2 3 4 5 6 7
10. Corporations don't give much feedback to WBEs.   1 2 3 4 5 6 7
11. Sexism is prevalent in corporations doing business with WBEs.   1 2 3 4 5 6 7
12. Obtaining required insurance is a problem for WBEs.   1 2 3 4 5 6 7
13. Corporations take too long to pay.   1 2 3 4 5 6 7
14. It's difficult for WBEs to get their foot in the door.   1 2 3 4 5 6 7
15. WBEs are often undercapitalized.   1 2 3 4 5 6 7
16. There is a lack of corporate commitment to WBE purchasing programs.   1 2 3 4 5 6 7
17. WBEs are powerless to negotiate favorable terms.   1 2 3 4 5 6 7
18. Buyers rely on their "old-boy networks" in selecting suppliers.   1 2 3 4 5 6 7
19. Only small-volume orders are placed with WBEs.   1 2 3 4 5 6 7
20. The government doesn't enforce the regulations on WBE purchasing.   1 2 3 4 5 6 7
21. WBEs are not available in specialized areas.   1 2 3 4 5 6 7
22. Buyers are not aware of available WBEs.   1 2 3 4 5 6 7
23. WBEs are not price-competitive.   1 2 3 4 5 6 7
24. Buyers lack information on WBE capability.   1 2 3 4 5 6 7
25. WBEs can't meet bid/quote deadlines.   1 2 3 4 5 6 7
26. Buyers have no incentive to make WBE purchasing programs work.   1 2 3 4 5 6 7
27. WBEs have a "give-me" attitude.   1 2 3 4 5 6 7
28. The WBE purchasing program is all politics.   1 2 3 4 5 6 7
29. Performance by WBEs is too uncertain.   1 2 3 4 5 6 7
30. WBEs have poor bidding practices.   1 2 3 4 5 6 7
31. Buyers have negative attitudes toward WBEs.   1 2 3 4 5 6 7
32. Resources to develop WBEs into reliable suppliers are not available.   1 2 3 4 5 6 7
33. Identifying and qualifying WBEs is a costly process.   1 2 3 4 5 6 7
34. Buyer turnover is too high to establish long-term relationships
    with WBEs.   1 2 3 4 5 6 7
35. WBE programs lead buyers to compromise their professional standards.   1 2 3 4 5 6 7
36. WBEs could be acting as a "front" for non-women business.   1 2 3 4 5 6 7
37. WBEs lack qualified technical personnel.   1 2 3 4 5 6 7
38. WBEs lack qualified managerial personnel.   1 2 3 4 5 6 7
39. WBEs lack qualified sales personnel.   1 2 3 4 5 6 7
40. WBEs have inefficient production capacities.   1 2 3 4 5 6 7
41. WBEs need long lead times to correct quality problems.   1 2 3 4 5 6 7

Instructions: Below is a list of activities that large companies might use to implement aspects of Women Business Enterprise (WBE) purchasing programs. Read each statement carefully and think about your own company. Then indicate whether you (1) **Strongly Disagree**, (2) **Moderately Disagree**, (3) **Slightly Disagree**, (4) **Neither Agree nor Disagree**, (5) **Slightly Agree**, (6) **Moderately Agree**, or (7) **Strongly Agree** that the activity should be part of a **large company's WBE program**.

1 Strongly Disagree	2 Moderately Disagree	3 Slightly Disagree	4 Neither Agree Nor Disagree	5 Slightly Agree	6 Moderately Agree	7 Strongly Agree

1. Provide or use a certification process. 1 2 3 4 5 6 7
2. Offer management assistance. 1 2 3 4 5 6 7
3. Participate in joint ventures. 1 2 3 4 5 6 7
4. Give WBEs access to company technical resources. 1 2 3 4 5 6 7
5. Make company internal training available to WBEs. 1 2 3 4 5 6 7
6. Hold quality assurance meetings. 1 2 3 4 5 6 7
7. Offer loans or loan guarantees to WBEs. 1 2 3 4 5 6 7
8. Attend trade fairs for WBEs. 1 2 3 4 5 6 7
9. Place ads in women's entrepreneur publications. 1 2 3 4 5 6 7
10. Establish prepayment agreements. 1 2 3 4 5 6 7
11. Waive restrictive requirements. 1 2 3 4 5 6 7
12. Employ automated monitoring/tracking of WBE agreements. 1 2 3 4 5 6 7
13. Help with bid preparation and simplify the bidding process. 1 2 3 4 5 6 7
14. Train buyers in problems of WBEs. 1 2 3 4 5 6 7
15. Require performance bonds. 1 2 3 4 5 6 7
16. Perform credit checks/reference checks. 1 2 3 4 5 6 7
17. Set specific purchasing target goals for WBEs. 1 2 3 4 5 6 7
18. Establish a WBE advocate program within the company. 1 2 3 4 5 6 7
19. High visibility and commendations for buyer participation. 1 2 3 4 5 6 7
20. Get top management involved. 1 2 3 4 5 6 7
21. Organize a permanent in-house task force.
22. Take a leadership role in community economic development regarding women in business. 1 2 3 4 5 6 7
23. Establish a WBE program in every department. 1 2 3 4 5 6 7
24. Employ automated data bases for WBE procurement and make a listing available to all departments.
25. Disseminate long-term purchasing needs. 1 2 3 4 5 6 7
26. Provide feedback to unsuccessful bidders. 1 2 3 4 5 6 7
27. Publish a list of buyer names/commodities and supply procedures. 1 2 3 4 5 6 7
28. List large-volume opportunities. 1 2 3 4 5 6 7

Job Title: _____Owner; Other (please specify)_____

Years in Current Position: _____

Race/Origin: _____Black _____Hispanic _____Caucasian _____Asian _____Nat. American

Level of Education: _____less than high school _____high school graduate

_____some college _____college degree

_____some graduate work _____graduate degree

What percentage of your sales is due to being a Women Business Enterprise? _____%

Approximate total annual sales, 1988: (check one)

_____less than $100,000 _____$100,000 to $499,999 _____$500,000 to $999,999

_____$1 million to $5 million _____more than $5 million

WOMEN BUSINESS ENTERPRISE PURCHASING PROGRAM SURVEY

Instructions: Below is a list of statements that may be used to describe problems facing Women Business Enterprise (WBE) purchasing programs. Read each statement carefully and think about your own company. Then indicate whether you (1) Strongly Disagree, (2) Moderately Disagree, (3) Slightly Disagree, (4) Neither Agree nor Disagree, (5) Slightly Agree, (6) Moderately Agree, or (7) Strongly Agree with the statement by circling the appropriate number.

1	2	3	4	5	6	7
Strongly Disagree	Moderately Disagree	Slightly Disagree	Neither Agree Nor Disagree	Slightly Agree	Moderately Agree	Strongly Agree

1. Doing business with large corporations is not very profitable for WBEs.
2. WBEs have difficulty advertising their products/services.   1 2 3 4 5 6 7
3. Corporations don't get the word out about their programs.   1 2 3 4 5 6 7
4. The designation of "women business" hurts WBEs.   1 2 3 4 5 6 7
5. WBEs can't compete with bigger firms.   1 2 3 4 5 6 7
6. Buyers don't know much about WBEs' business.   1 2 3 4 5 6 7
7. WBEs need technical assistance.   1 2 3 4 5 6 7
8. Buyers use WBEs just to satisfy statistics.   1 2 3 4 5 6 7
9. Buyers don't work closely with WBEs.   1 2 3 4 5 6 7
10. Corporations don't give much feedback to WBEs.   1 2 3 4 5 6 7
11. Sexism is prevalent in corporations doing business with WBEs.   1 2 3 4 5 6 7
12. Obtaining required insurance is a problem for WBEs.   1 2 3 4 5 6 7
13. Corporations take too long to pay.   1 2 3 4 5 6 7
14. It's difficult for WBEs to get their foot in the door.   1 2 3 4 5 6 7
15. WBEs are often undercapitalized.   1 2 3 4 5 6 7
16. There is a lack of corporate commitment to WBE purchasing programs.   1 2 3 4 5 6 7
17. WBEs are powerless to negotiate favorable terms.   1 2 3 4 5 6 7
18. Buyers rely on their "old boy networks" in selecting suppliers.   1 2 3 4 5 6 7
19. Only small-volume orders are placed with WBEs.   1 2 3 4 5 6 7
20. The government doesn't enforce the regulations on WBE purchasing.   1 2 3 4 5 6 7
21. WBEs are not available in specialized areas.   1 2 3 4 5 6 7
22. Buyers are not aware of available WBEs.   1 2 3 4 5 6 7
23. WBEs are not price-competitive.   1 2 3 4 5 6 7
24. Buyers lack information on WBE capability.   1 2 3 4 5 6 7
25. WBEs can't meet bid/quote deadlines.   1 2 3 4 5 6 7
26. Buyers have no incentive to make WBE purchasing programs work.   1 2 3 4 5 6 7
27. WBEs have a "give-me" attitude.   1 2 3 4 5 6 7
28. The WBE purchasing program is all politics.   1 2 3 4 5 6 7
29. Performance by WBEs is too uncertain.   1 2 3 4 5 6 7
30. WBEs have poor bidding practices.   1 2 3 4 5 6 7
31. Buyers have negative attitudes toward WBEs.   1 2 3 4 5 6 7
32. Resources to develop WBEs into reliable suppliers are not available. 1 2 3 4 5 6 7
33. Identifying and qualifying WBEs is a costly process.   1 2 3 4 5 6 7
34. Buyer turnover is too high to establish long-term relationships with WBEs.   1 2 3 4 5 6 7
35. WBE programs lead buyers to compromise their professional standards. 1 2 3 4 5 6 7
36. WBEs could be acting as a "front" for non-women business.   1 2 3 4 5 6 7
37. WBEs lack qualified technical personnel.   1 2 3 4 5 6 7
38. WBEs lack qualified managerial personnel.   1 2 3 4 5 6 7
39. WBEs lack qualified sales personnel.   1 2 3 4 5 6 7
40. WBEs have inefficient production capacities.   1 2 3 4 5 6 7
41. WBEs need long lead times to correct quality problems.   1 2 3 4 5 6 7

Instructions: Below is a list of activities that large companies might use to implement aspects of Women Business Enterprise (WBE) purchasing programs. Read each statement carefully and think about your own company. Then indicate whether you (1) **Strongly Disagree**, (2) **Moderately Disagree**, (3) **Slightly Disagree**, (4) **Neither Agree nor Disagree**, (5) **Slightly Agree**, (6) **Moderately Agree**, or (7) **Strongly Agree** that the activity should be part of a large company's WBE program.

1 Strongly Disagree	2 Moderately Disagree	3 Slightly Disagree	4 Neither Agree Nor Disagree	5 Slightly Agree	6 Moderately Agree	7 Strongly Agree

1. Provide or use a certification process.   1 2 3 4 5 6 7
2. Offer management assistance.   1 2 3 4 5 6 7
3. Participate in joint ventures.   1 2 3 4 5 6 7
4. Give WBEs access to company technical resources.   1 2 3 4 5 6 7
5. Make company internal training available to WBEs.   1 2 3 4 5 6 7
6. Hold quality assurance meetings.   1 2 3 4 5 6 7
7. Offer loans or loan guarantees to WBEs.   1 2 3 4 5 6 7
8. Attend trade fairs for WBEs.   1 2 3 4 5 6 7
9. Place ads in women's entrepreneur publications.   1 2 3 4 5 6 7
10. Establish prepayment agreements.   1 2 3 4 5 6 7
11. Waive restrictive requirements.   1 2 3 4 5 6 7
12. Employ automated monitoring/tracking of WBE agreements.   1 2 3 4 5 6 7
13. Help with bid preparation and simplify the bidding process.   1 2 3 4 5 6 7
14. Train buyers in problems of WBEs.   1 2 3 4 5 6 7
15. Require performance bonds.   1 2 3 4 5 6 7
16. Perform credit checks/reference checks.   1 2 3 4 5 6 7
17. Set specific purchasing target goals for WBEs.   1 2 3 4 5 6 7
18. Establish a WBE advocate program within the company.   1 2 3 4 5 6 7
19. High visibility and commendations for buyer participation.   1 2 3 4 5 6 7
20. Get top management involved.   1 2 3 4 5 6 7
21. Organize a permanent in-house task force.   1 2 3 4 5 6 7
22. Take a leadership role in community economic development regarding women in business.   1 2 3 4 5 6 7
23. Establish a WBE program in every department.   1 2 3 4 5 6 7
24. Employ automated data bases for WBE procurement and make a listing available to all departments.   1 2 3 4 5 6 7
25. Disseminate long-term purchasing needs.   1 2 3 4 5 6 7
26. Provide feedback to unsuccessful bidders.   1 2 3 4 5 6 7
27. Publish a list of buyer names/commodities and supply procedures.   1 2 3 4 5 6 7
28. List large volume opportunities.   1 2 3 4 5 6 7

Your Job Title_____

Years in Current Position_____

Race/Origin: _____Black _____Hispanic _____Caucasian _____Asian _____Nat. American

Level of Education: _____less than high school _____high school graduate

_____some college _____college degree

_____some graduate work _____graduate degree

What percentage of your total purchasing dollars spent is allocated to Women Business Enterprises? _____%

Approximate total annual sales, 1988: (check one)

_____less than $500 million _____$500 million to $1 billion

_____$1,000,000,001 to $5 billion _____$5,000,000,001 to $10 billion

_____more than $10 billion

APPENDIX B: RANK ORDER OF IMPEDIMENTS AND ACTIVITIES AS PERCEIVED BY WBEs AND CPPs: COMPLETE LISTS •

RANK ORDER OF IMPEDIMENTS AS PERCEIVED BY WBEs: COMPLETE LIST

Rank	Item	Mean Score of Impediment Item	Variable*
1	WBEs are often undercapitalized.	5.813	Resource Dependence
2	Buyers rely on their "old-boy networks" in selecting suppliers.	5.716	Opportunism
3	It's difficult for WBEs to get their foot in the door.	5.541	Atmosphere
4	Buyers lack information on WBE capability.	5.459	Impacted Information
5	Buyers use WBEs just to satisfy statistics.	5.419	Opportunism
6	Only small-volume orders are placed with WBEs.	5.351	Resource Dependence
7	There is a lack of corporate commitment to WBE purchasing programs.	5.351	Opportunism
8	Buyers don't know much about WBEs' business.	5.329	Impacted Information/ Bounded Rationality (Complexity)
9	Corporations take too long to pay.	5.205	Resource Dependence
10	Buyers don't work closely with WBEs.	5.205	Atmosphere
11	Corporations don't get the word out about their programs.	5.200	Impacted Information
12	Buyers are not aware of available WBEs.	5.149	Few Firms
13	The government doesn't enforce the regulations on WBE purchasing.	5.108	Bounded Rationality (Complexity)
14	Buyers have no incentive to make WBE purchasing programs work.	5.027	Bounded Rationality (Complexity)
15	Corporations don't give much feedback to WBEs.	4.986	Resource Dependence
16	Buyers have negative attitudes toward WBEs.	4.973	Atmosphere
17	WBEs can't compete with bigger firms.	4.932	Resource Dependence
18	Sexism is prevalent in corporations doing business with WBEs.	4.824	Atmosphere
19	Resources to develop WBEs into reliable suppliers are not available.	4.757	Impacted Information
20	The WBE purchasing program is all politics.	4.575	Opportunism
21	WBEs need technical assistance.	4.573	Resource Dependence
22	Obtaining required insurance is a problem for WBEs.	4.397	Business Uncertainty
23	The designation of "women business" hurts WBEs.	4.311	Atmosphere
24	WBEs could be acting as a "front" for non-women business.	4.274	Opportunism
25	Identifying and qualifying WBEs is a costly process.	4.257	Few Firms
26	WBEs are powerless to negotiate favorable terms.	4.080	Resource Dependence
27	WBEs have difficulty advertising their products/services.	4.042	Impacted Information
28	Doing business with large corporations is not very profitable for WBEs.	4.000	Business Uncertainty
29	WBEs are not available in specialized areas.	3.986	Few Firms
30	Buyer turnover is too high to establish long-term relationships with WBEs.	3.784	Bounded Rationality (Complexity)
31	WBEs are not price-competitive.	3.233	Business Uncertainty
32	WBEs have a "give-me" attitude.	3.139	Opportunism
33	WBE programs lead buyers to compromise their professional standards.	3.027	Bounded Rationality (Complexity)
34	WBEs have poor bidding practices.	2.905	Bounded Rationality (Complexity)
35	Performance by WBEs is too uncertain.	2.662	Business Uncertainty
36	WBEs lack qualified technical personnel.	2.581	Production Uncertainty
37	WBEs lack qualified managerial personnel.	2.568	Business Uncertainty
38	WBEs lack qualified sales personnel.	2.514	Business Uncertainty
39	WBEs can't meet bid/quote deadlines.	2.479	Business Uncertainty
40	WBEs have inefficient production capacities.	2.405	Production Uncertainty
41	WBEs need long lead times to correct quality problems.	2.257	Production Uncertainty

*Variables were created out of the items in the survey instrument to represent the dimensions of the transaction-cost framework.

RANK ORDER OF IMPEDIMENTS AS PERCEIVED BY CPPs: COMPLETE LIST

Rank	Item	Mean Score of Impediment Item	Variable*
1	Buyers are not aware of available WBEs.	4.857	Few Firms
2	WBEs are not available in specialized areas.	4.848	Few Firms
3	Buyers lack information on WBE capability.	4.705	Impacted Information
4	WBEs are often undercapitalized.	4.610	Resource Dependence
5	Buyers don't know much about WBEs' business.	4.381	Impacted Information/ Bounded Rationality (Complexity)
6	Corporations don't get the word out about their programs.	4.324	Impacted Information
7	WBEs could be acting as a "front" for non-women business.	4.324	Opportunism
8	WBEs need technical assistance.	4.152	Resource Dependence
9	There is a lack of corporate commitment to WBE purchasing programs.	4.126	Opportunism
10	The government doesn't enforce the regulations onWBE purchasing.	4.097	Bounded Rationality (Complexity)
11	Identifying and qualifying WBEs is a costly process.	4.010	Few Firms
12	Buyers have no incentive to make WBE purchasing programs work.	3.905	Bounded Rationality (Complexity)
13	Corporations don't give much feedback to WBEs.	3.857	Resource Dependence
14	It's difficult for WBEs to get their foot in the door.	3.781	Atmosphere
15	Resources to develop WBEs into reliable suppliers are not available.	3.743	Impacted Information
16	Obtaining required insurance is a problem for WBEs.	3.709	Business Uncertainty
17	Corporations take too long to pay.	3.686	Resource Dependence
18	Only small-volume orders are placed with WBEs.	3.638	Resource Dependence
19	WBEs lack qualified technical personnel.	3.610	Production Uncertainty
20	WBEs are not price-competitive.	3.569	Business Uncertainty
21	WBEs have a "give-me" attitude.	3.543	Opportunism
22	Buyers don't work closely with WBEs.	3.519	Atmosphere
23	WBEs have inefficient production capacities.	3.490	Production Uncertainty
24	Buyers rely on their "old-boy netorks" in selecting suppliers.	3.343	Opportunism
25	The WBE purchasing program is all politics.	3.317	Opportunism
26	Buyers use WBEs just to satisfy statistics.	3.314	Opportunism
27	WBEs lack qualified sales personnel.	3.276	Business Uncertainty
28	WBEs lack qualified managerial personnel.	3.276	Business Uncertainty
29	WBEs can't compete with bigger firms.	3.276	Resource Dependence
30	The designation of "women business" hurts WBEs.	3.229	Atmosphere
31	Buyers have negative attitudes toward WBEs.	3.221	Atmosphere
32	WBEs have difficulty advertising their products/services.	3.087	Impacted Information
33	Performance by WBEs is too uncertain.	3.057	Business Uncertainty
34	WBEs need long lead times to correct quality problems.	3.048	Production Uncertainty
35	WBEs have poor bidding practices.	3.010	Bounded Rationality (Complexity)
36	WBEs can't meet bid/quote deadlines.	2.635	Business Uncertainty
37	Sexism is prevalent in corporations doing business with WBEs.	2.600	Atmosphere
38	Buyer turnover is too high to establish long-term relationships with WBEs.	2.598	Bounded Rationality (Complexity)
39	Doing business with large corporationsis not very profitable for WBEs.	2.500	Business Uncertainty
40	WBEs are powerless to negotiate favorable terms.	2.362	Resource Dependence
41	WBE programs lead buyers to compromise their professional standards.	2.163	Bounded Rationality (Complexity)

*Variables were created out of the items in the survey instrument to represent the dimensions of the transaction-cost framework.

RANK ORDER OF ACTIVITIES AS PERCEIVED BY WBEs: COMPLETE LIST

Rank	Item	Mean Score of Activity Item	Variable*
1	List large-volume opportunities.	5.886	Searching for CPPs
2	Provide feedback to unsuccessful bidders.	5.871	Managerial Assistance
3	Get top management involved.	5.845	Monitoring of CPPs
4	Publish a list of buyer names/commodities and supply procedures.	5.671	Searching for CPPs
5	High visibility and commendations for buyer participation.	5.634	Monitoring of CPPs
6	Take a leadership role in community economic development regarding women in business.	5.609	Searching for CPPs
7	Disseminate long-term purchasing needs.	5.551	Searching for CPPs
8	Employ automated data bases for WBE procurement and make a listing available to all departments.	5.471	Searching for WBEs
9	Participate in joint ventures.	5.366	Internalization
10	Establish a WBE advocate program within the company.	5.342	Monitoring of CPPs
11	Attend trade fairs for WBEs.	5.268	Searching for WBEs
12	Hold quality assurance meetings.	5.246	Monitoring of WBEs
13	Train buyers in problems of WBEs.	5.239	Monitoring of WBEs/ Cultural Interaction
14	Provide or use a certification process.	5.214	Managerial Assistance
15	Perform credit checks/reference checks.	5.214	Monitoring of WBEs
16	Set specific purchasing target goals for WBEs.	5.211	Monitoring of CPPS
17	Give WBEs access to company technical resources.	5.197	Technical Assistance/ Internalization
18	Place ads in women's entrepreneur publications.	5.186	Searching for WBEs
19	Establish prepayment agreements.	5.186	Financial Assistance
20	Help with bid preparation and simplify the bidding process.	5.155	Searching for WBEs/ Technical Assistance
21	Offer management assistance.	5.042	Managerial Assistance
22	Offer loans or loan guarantees to WBEs.	5.000	Financial Assistance
23	Make company internal training available to WBEs.	4.972	Internalization
24	Organize a permanent in-house task force.	4.918	Monitoring of CPPs
25	Establish a WBE program in every department.	4.592	Monitoring of CPPs
26	Waive restrictive requirements.	4.500	Searching for WBEs
27	Employ automated monitoring/tracking of WBE agreements.	4.431	Monitoring of CPPs
28	Require performance bonds.	3.845	Monitoring of WBEs

*Variables were created out of the items in the survey instrument to represent the dimensions of the transaction-cost framework.

RANK ORDER OF ACTIVITIES AS PERCEIVED BY CPPs: COMPLETE LIST

Rank	Item	Mean Score of Activity Item	Variable*
1	Provide feedback to unsuccessful bidders.	5.820	Managerial Assistance
2	Publish a list of buyer names/commodities and supply procedures.	5.782	Searching for CPPs
3	Attend trade fairs for WBEs.	5.644	Searching for WBEs
4	Hold quality assurance meetings.	5.621	Monitoring of WBEs
5	Perform credit checks/reference checks.	5.304	Monitoring of WBEs
6	Provide or use a certification process.	5.284	Managerial Assistance
7	List large-volume opportunities.	5.059	Searching for CPPs
8	Train buyers in problems of WBEs.	5.038	Monitoring of WBEs/ Cultural Interaction
9	Get top management involved.	4.971	Monitoring of CPPs
10	Disseminate long-term purchasing needs.	4.971	Searching for CPPs
11	High visibility and commendations for buyer participation.	4.524	Monitoring of CPPs
12	Employ automated data bases for WBE procurement and make a listing available to all departments.	4.433	Searching for WBEs
13	Set specific purchasing target goals for WBEs.	4.417	Monitoring of CPPS
14	Take a leadership role in community economic development regarding women in business.	4.373	Searching for CPPs
15	Offer management assistance.	4.350	Managerial Assistance
16	Establish a WBE advocate program within the company.	4.350	Monitoring of CPPs
17	Give WBEs access to company technical resources.	4.291	Technical Assistance/ Internalization
18	Place ads in women's entrepreneur publications.	4.233	Searching for WBEs
19	Employ automated monitoring/tracking of WBE agreements.	4.155	Monitoring of CPPs
20	Help with bid preparation and simplify the bidding process.	3.990	Searching for WBEs/ Technical Assistance
21	Participate in joint ventures.	3.971	Internalization
22	Make company internal training available to WBEs.	3.777	Internalization
23	Require performance bonds.	3.602	Monitoring of WBEs
24	Organize a permanent in-house task force.	3.539	Monitoring of CPPs
25	Establish prepayment agreements.	3.431	Financial Assistance
26	Establish a WBE program in every department.	3.282	Monitoring of CPPs
27	Offer loans or loan guarantees to WBEs.	2.755	Financial Assistance
28	Waive restrictive requirements.	2.650	Searching for WBEs

*Variables were created out of the items in the survey instrument to represent the dimensions of the transaction-cost framework.

CENTER FOR ADVANCED PURCHASING STUDIES •

THE CENTER FOR ADVANCED PURCHASING STUDIES (CAPS) was established in November 1986 as an affiliation agreement between the College of Business at Arizona State University and the National Association of Purchasing Management. It is located at The Arizona State University Research Park, 2055 East Centennial Circle, P.O. Box 22160, Tempe, Arizona 85285-2160 (Telephone [602] 752-2277).

The Center has three major goals to be accomplished through its research program:

- to improve purchasing effectiveness and efficiency;
- to improve overall purchasing capability;
- to increase the competitiveness of U.S. companies in a global economy.

Research under way and planned includes Global Purchasing; World-Class Purchasing Organizations and Practices to 1995; Purchasing Benchmarking; Purchasing Education and Training Requirements and Resources; the Quality Issue; and Purchasing's Involvement in Transportation Decision Making.

CAPS, a 501 (c) (3) not-for-profit research organization, is funded solely by tax-deductible contributions from corporations and individuals who want to make a difference in the state of purchasing and materials management knowledge. Policy guidance is provided by the Board of Trustees consisting of:

R. Jerry Baker, C.P.M., the National Association of Purchasing Management
William A. Bales, C.P.M., Union Pacific Railroad and the National Association of Purchasing Management
William Bothwell, Northern Telecom Inc.
John Cologna, C.P.M., General Electric Company
Montague E. Cooper, C.P.M., Chevron U.S.A. Inc.
Harold E. Fearon, Ph.D., C.P.M., the Center for Advanced Purchasing Studies and Arizona State University
Lowell Hoffman, Colgate-Palmolive Company
Michael G. Kolchin, Ph.D., C.P.M., Lehigh University
Donna Lynes, C.P.M., Arcop, Inc.
Robert R. Paul, Lockheed Corporation

The Center for Advanced Purchasing Studies and the National Association of Purchasing Management wish to thank the following corporations, foundations, individuals, and affiliated purchasing management associations for their financial support:

CORPORATIONS/FOUNDATIONS

$40,000 and Over
BellSouth Services
Northern Telecom Inc.
U S WEST Business Resources, Inc.

$20,000 and Over
ARCO
BP America
Chevron U.S.A. Inc.
Conoco/Du Pont
RJR Nabisco, Inc.
Texas Instruments Incorporated
TRW Foundation
Westinghouse Foundation

$10,000 and Over
AT&T
Carnival Cruise Lines
Caterpillar Inc.
CSX Transportation
Eastman Kodak Company
G.E. Company, Corporate Sourcing
Kraft, Inc.
Lockheed Leadership Fund
Mobil Foundation
Polaroid Corporation
Raytheon Company
Shell Oil Company
Texaco Services, Inc.
Union Pacific Railroad Corporation
UNISYS Corporation

$5,000 and Over
Amoco Corporation
Corning Incorporated
Distribution Magazine—A Chilton Company
Exxon Company, U.S.A.
Firestone Trust Fund
The HCA Foundation
Hughes Aircraft
Intel Corporation
NYNEX Materiel Enterprises Company

37

CORPORATIONS/FOUNDATIONS (continued)

Phillips Petroleum Company
Southern Pacific Transportation Co.
United Technologies Corporation

$4,999 and Under
The American Tobacco Co.
Americhem Inc.
Ameritech Services
ANR Freight Systems, Inc.
Arcop, Inc.
ARGO-TECH Corporation
Avery, Materials Group
Barnes Group Foundation
The Bauer Group
Carter Chemicals & Services, Inc.
C.M. Almy & Sons, Inc.
Coastal Savings Bank
Concord Realstate Corp.

Dragon Products Co.
Ernst & Young
Freeway Corporation
G.E. Company,
   Contracting/Purchasing
The Glidden Company
Haluch & Associates
Imperial Litho/Graphics, Inc.
Industrial Distribution Association
International Minerals &
   Chemicals Corporation
Keithley Instruments, Inc.
The Lincoln Electric Company
Loctite Corporation
L-Tec Welding & Cutting Systems
Marathon Oil Company
N.I.G.P., Arizona State Capitol Chapter
North Canton Tool Company

Oatey Company
Ohio Power Company
Olin Corporation
   Charitable Trust
ORYX Energy Company
OXY USA Inc.
Pacific Bell
Parker Hannifin Corporation
Pharmaceutical Manufacturers
   Association
The Quality Castings Co.
Restaurants & Institutions
Reznor
Shamrock Hose & Fitting Company
Simmons Precision Product Inc.
Society Corporation
Union Camp Corporation
The Upjohn Company

AFFILIATED ASSOCIATIONS

Akron, Inc.
Arkansas
Bay Area
Boston
Canton
Cincinnati, Inc.
Cleveland
Dallas
Dayton
Delaware
Denver, Inc.
Detroit, Inc.
District VI
District VII
District IX
Florida Central
Florida First Coast
Florida Gold Coast
Florida Space Coast
Florida West Coast
Fox Valley, Wisconsin
Georgia

Iowa (Central)
Iowa (Eastern)
Kansas City
Lehigh Valley, Inc.
Lima Area, Inc.
Madison Area
Maine
Maryland, Inc.
Memphis
Michigan (Western)
Milwaukee
New Jersey
New Mexico
New Orleans, Inc.
Oklahoma City
Old Dominion, Inc. (Virginia)
Oregon
Northeastern PA
Northwestern Pennsylvania, Inc.
North Central
Petroleum Industry Buyers Group
Philadelphia Inc.

Pittsburgh, PA
Rhode Island
Sabine-Neches
Southern Arizona, Inc.
Southwestern Michigan, Inc.
Spokane
Springfield, Inc.
St. Louis
Syracuse and Central New York, Inc.
Tennessee (East)
Tenneva
Toledo Area, Inc.
Transportation Group
Treasure Valley
Tulsa, Inc.
Twin City
Washington (D.C.)
Western Colorado, Inc.
Western Michigan, Inc.
Youngstown District (Ohio)

INDIVIDUALS

R. Jerry Baker, C.P.M.
William A. Bales, C.P.M.
Diane K. Bishop
Joseph T. Boylan
Robert Breitbart
Patricia G. Cole
Gerard R. Coiley, Sr.
Montague E. Cooper, C.P.M.
Frank Croyl
Walter Eads
Julius Edelmann
Harold E. Fearon, Ph.D., C.P.M.
Ted D. Hadley

John H. Hoagland, Ph.D., C.P.M.
Joan Humphrey, C.P.M.
Richard Lee Jackson, C.P.M.
Robert L. Janson, C.P.M.
Robert Kaminski, C.P.M.
Dr. Kenneth H. Killen
Arnold Lovering, C.P.M.
Frederick W. Ludwig
Walter Mielcarek, C.P.M.
Paul K. Moffat, C.P.M.
Thomas A. Nash, C.P.M.
John P. Negrelli
R.D. Nelson

Robert P. Olson, C.P.M.
Harold F. Puff, Ph.D., C.P.M.
Jon E. Schmiedebusch
Stanley N. Sherman, Ph.D., C.P.M.
Jonathan R. Stegner
Scott Sturzl, C.P.M.
Arthur W. Todd
Dennis Urbonas
Robert F. Weber
Milton Welch
W.A. Westerbeck
Elaine Whittington, C.P.M.
Mr. & Mrs. Harry B. Wiggins

CENTER FOR ADVANCED PURCHASING STUDIES
Arizona State University Research Park
2055 East Centennial Circle
P.O. Box 22160
Tempe, Arizona 85285-2160
(602) 752-2277

ISBN: 0-945968-05-1